A Teenager's Guide to

# The Invisible

# Creation

## A Peek into God's Supernatural Realm

by Jerry Ross

To order additional copies:
*www.stayinthecastle.com*
or call (812)665-4375

*A Teenager's Guide to*

# The Invisible Creation

A Peek into God's Supernatural Realm

# Other Books by the Author

*Stay in the Castle*

*Seven Royal Laws of Courtship*

*The Teenage Years of Jesus Christ*

*The Childhood Years of Jesus Christ*

*The 21 Tenets of Biblical Femininity*

*The 21 Tenets of Biblical Masculinity*

*Is Your Youth Group Dead or Alive?*

*Mountain Lessons*

*Grace Will Lead Me Home*

*104 Teen Bible Lessons*

*Did God Put a Book Inside of You?*

# The Teenager's Guide Series

*A Teenager's Guide to*
*Character, Success & Happiness*

*A Teenager's Guide to the Invisible Creation*

*A Teenager's Guide to Healthy Relationships*

# Table of Contents

**2 Corinthians 4:18**
*While we look not at the things which are seen,*
*but at the things which are not seen:*
*for the things which are seen are temporal;*
*but the things which are not seen are eternal.*

# INTRODUCTION

A study into God's invisible creation is not for the faint of heart. Everything visible constantly screams for our attention, yet the invisible is infinitely more important than the visible. Every Christian needs to see what the world ignores.

All who have passed on now believe. They believe because they now see it. But for those of us who believe by faith what the Bible teaches, we must believe before we see. And because of this, we are blessed.

*John 20:29, Jesus saith unto him, Thomas, because thou hast seen me, thou hast believed: blessed are they that have not seen, and yet have believed.*

Study carefully the chapters ahead. Do so with an open Bible and, above all, be blessed.

Jerry Ross

**Colossians 1:16**
*For by him (Jesus) were all things created,*
*that are in heaven, and that are in earth,*
***visible and invisible,***
*whether they be thrones, or dominions,*
*or principalities, or powers:*
*all things were created by him, and for him:*

# -1-
# Our Invisible God

*True worship is when man's invisible spirit meets with the invisible God.  — Unknown*

## Lesson Goals
1. To understand the two reasons God remains invisible
2. To examine Moses' interaction with God
3. To see how an encounter with God can transform us

## The Visible and the Invisible Creation
*Colossians 1:12-17 ...For by him were all things created, that are in heaven, and that are in earth, visible and invisible,* whether they be thrones, or dominions, or principalities, or powers: all things were created by him, and for him:  And he is before all things, and by him all things consist.

When God the Creator made this earth, His creation was divided into two categories:  things we can see and things we cannot.   There is a creation that is visible to mortal men, and a creation that is invisible to mortal men.   Although the invisible creation cannot be seen, God has given us information in the Bible about what exists beyond our vision.

## Why an Invisible Creation?

Faith is important to God.  He insists that any relationship He has with man be based on faith.
*Romans 1:17  For therein is the righteousness of God revealed from faith to faith: as it is written, The just shall live by faith.*

***Galatians 3:11*** *But that no man is justified by the law in the sight of God, it is evident: for, The just shall live by faith.*

***Ephesians 6:16*** *Above all, taking the shield of faith, wherewith ye shall be able to quench all the fiery darts of the wicked.*

***Hebrews 11:1-6*** *Now faith is the substance of things hoped for, the evidence of things not seen.... Through faith we understand that the worlds were framed by the word of God, so that things which are seen were not made of things which do appear.... But without faith it is impossible to please him: for he that cometh to God must believe that he is, and that he is a rewarder of them that diligently seek him.*

No man can be saved without faith. No Christian can please God without faith. Faith is the *"evidence of things not seen."* If you decide that you are going to refuse to believe anything that you cannot see or prove, then you will never be saved. Faith is vital in our relationship with God.

## God is Invisible

***Colossians 1:15*** *Who is the image of the invisible God, the firstborn of every creature:*

***1 Timothy 1:17*** *Now unto the King eternal, immortal, invisible, the only wise God, be honour and glory for ever and ever. Amen.*

God created the invisible creation. He also is the invisible Creator. Again, He chooses to remain unseen by men so that our relationship with Him is founded on faith.

"Well, if God wants us to believe in Him, then why doesn't He just show Himself to us, face to face?" He will not do that for two reasons:

1. Because that would nullify the need for faith.
2. Because you wouldn't live to tell about it!

## No Man Has Seen God's Face

God has never revealed Himself to man in all of His power and glory. No man has ever seen the "face" of God. It is impossible for mortal man to see God face to face and live. Moses probably came the closest to seeing God's fullness, but as we will see, even then God had to protect Moses by only allowing him to see part of God's presence.

*Exodus 19:20-25* *And the LORD came down upon mount Sinai, on the top of the mount: and the LORD called Moses up to the top of the mount; and Moses went up.* ***And the LORD said unto Moses, Go down, charge the people, lest they break through unto the LORD to gaze, and many of them perish.*** *And let the priests also, which come near to the LORD, sanctify themselves, lest the LORD break forth upon them. And Moses said unto the LORD, The people cannot come up to mount Sinai: for thou chargedst us, saying, Set bounds about the mount, and sanctify it. And the LORD said unto him, Away, get thee down, and thou shalt come up, thou, and Aaron with thee: but let not the priests and the people break through to come up unto the LORD, lest he break forth upon them. So Moses went down unto the people, and spake unto them.*

Although the presence of God was revealed to the people as He descended upon Mt. Sinai, barriers were put up to prevent any of the people from breaking forth and seeing the fullness of God. If they had, they would have perished.

*Exodus 33:8-11* *And it came to pass, when Moses went out unto the tabernacle, that all the people rose up, and stood every man at his tent door, and looked af-*

*ter Moses, until he was gone into the tabernacle. And it came to pass, as Moses entered into the tabernacle, the cloudy pillar descended, and stood at the door of the tabernacle, and the LORD talked with Moses. And all the people saw the cloudy pillar stand at the tabernacle door: and all the people rose up and worshipped, every man in his tent door. **And the LORD spake unto Moses face to face**, as a man speaketh unto his friend...*

The phrase *"spake unto Moses face to face"* is a description of their communication, not a description of a face to face encounter. We know this is true by reading the verses that follow.

*Exodus 33:17-23 And the LORD said unto Moses, I will do this thing also that thou hast spoken: for thou hast found grace in my sight, and I know thee by name... **And he said, Thou canst not see my face: for there shall no man see me, and live.** And the LORD said, Behold, there is a place by me, and thou shalt stand upon a rock: And it shall come to pass, while my glory passeth by, that I will put thee in a clift of the rock, and will cover thee with my hand while I pass by: And I will take away mine hand, and thou shalt see my back parts: but my face shall not be seen.*

## A Life-Changing Encounter With God

What an amazing encounter! Can you imagine? Moses wanted so badly to see the Lord that God granted him his request. God put him in the cleft of a rock, covered Moses with His hand, passed by, and allowed Moses to see God's after-presence. Had Moses seen the full glory of the Lord, it would have killed him. So he saw instead his "back parts" or His after-glow. This was no small thing! Notice in the verses below the effect of this encounter.

*Exodus 34:29-35 And it came to pass, when Mo-*

*ses came down from mount Sinai with the two tables of testimony in Moses' hand,* **when he came down from the mount, that Moses wist not that the skin of his face shone** *while he talked with him.  And when Aaron and all the children of Israel saw Moses,* **behold, the skin of his face shone***; and they were afraid to come nigh him. And Moses called unto them; and Aaron and all the rulers of the congregation returned unto him: and Moses talked with them.  And afterward all the children of Israel came nigh: and he gave them in commandment all that the LORD had spoken with him in mount Sinai.* **And till Moses had done speaking with them, he put a vail on his face.   But when Moses went in before the LORD to speak with him, he took the vail off, until he came out.** *And he came out, and spake unto the children of Israel that which he was commanded.* **And the children of Israel saw the face of Moses, that the skin of Moses' face shone:** *and Moses put the vail upon his face again, until he went in to speak with him.*

Oh, to have such an encounter with God!  Are you willing to pay the price to have this kind of personal relationship with the Lord?  God promises to reveal Himself to those who really seek Him.

***Proverbs 8:17*** *I love them that love me; and those that seek me early shall find me.*

What was God's reward to Moses for being willing to seek Him?

## 1.  Moses was allowed to see the "hand of God."

***Exodus 33:22*** *And it shall come to pass, while my glory passeth by, that I will put thee in a clift of the rock, and will cover thee with my hand while I pass by:*

If God used His hand to shelter Moses, then Moses saw God's hand!  Have you ever heard a preacher use the phrase "the hand of God?"  Christians use this phrase when they have witnessed something divine and miraculous happen. As in, "You could see the hand of God in this," or "We really saw God's hand at work." Every Christian should long to see the miraculous! Those who pay the price to seek the presence of God will be rewarded by getting to see the hand of God.

## 2. Moses was allowed to see God in a new and powerful way.

*Exodus 19:20 And the LORD came down upon mount Sinai, on the top of the mount: and the LORD called Moses up to the top of the mount; and Moses went up.*

Every one of us from time to time needs to have a new, fresh encounter with God. One that allows us to know Him in a way we have not known before.

## 3. Moses' countenance was transformed by this encounter.

Sin affects our countenance!

*Genesis 4:5-6 But unto Cain and to his offering he had not respect. And Cain was very wroth, and his countenance fell. And the LORD said unto Cain, Why art thou wroth? and why is thy countenance fallen?*

Walking with God also affects our countenance. The condition of a person's heart is not long kept from his or her face. Spending time with God gives us a holy glow!

## 4. The people could see the difference in Moses.

Time alone with God changes us! This change is so dramatic that it is impossible to hide!

*Exodus 34:30 And when Aaron and all the children of Israel saw Moses, behold, the skin of his face shone; and they were afraid to come nigh him.*

Our God is an invisible God. Yet, He is willing to reveal Himself to those who will truly seek Him. In the next chapter, we will see how the Lord chooses to reveal Himself to us in this, the church age.

## Points to Ponder and Discuss

1. List and explain the two reasons God remains invisible to men today.

2. What part of Moses' encounter with God fascinates you the most?

3. Discuss the merits of this statement: "Every Christian is as close to God as he/she really wants to be."

# -2-
# Old Testament Appearances of God

*"Faith sees the invisible, believes the unbelievable, and receives the impossible."* — Corrie Ten Boom

**Lesson Goals**
1. To study the Old Testament appearances of God
2. To understand God better through these appearances
3. To see how people reacted to God's interaction with them

   ***Hebrews 11:24-27** By faith Moses, when he was come to years, refused to be called the son of Pharaoh's daughter; Choosing rather to suffer affliction with the people of God, than to enjoy the pleasures of sin for a season; Esteeming the reproach of Christ greater riches than the treasures in Egypt: for he had respect unto the recompence of the reward. By faith he forsook Egypt, not fearing the wrath of the king: **for he endured, as seeing him who is invisible**.*

   It is wonderful to study the Bible and to see how God has revealed Himself to mankind throughout history. Let's look back at the wonder of the Old Testament appearances, and then learn how God chooses to reveal Himself to us today.

## Old Testament Appearances of the Godhead
   God revealed Himself to men in a variety of ways in the Old Testament. Imagine, the Almighty interacting

with the mortal!  God has always desired for man to know Him, and has occasionally given mankind a peek at His powerful presence.  Here are a few examples:

## 1.  The Burning Bush

*Exodus 3:3-5*  *And Moses said, I will now turn aside, and see this great sight, why the bush is not burnt. And when the LORD saw that he turned aside to see, God called unto him out of the midst of the bush, and said, Moses, Moses. And he said, Here am I.  And he said, Draw not nigh hither: put off thy shoes from off thy feet, for the place whereon thou standest is holy ground.*

God appeared to Moses to enlist him in a divine calling.  God always has a purpose when He reveals Himself to man.  The children of Israel needed a deliverer.  Moses was God's choice to be the one to lead them out of the land of bondage.  God spoke to Moses out of the burning bush and revealed to him God's special calling.

God still personally enlists men to positions of spiritual leadership today.  No man can call another man to be a preacher.  God alone reserves this right to Himself.  Throughout time, God has called men to be pastors, preachers, evangelists and missionaries.

## 2.  Captain of the Host

*Joshua 5:13-15*  *And it came to pass, when Joshua was by Jericho, that he lifted up his eyes and looked, and, behold, there stood a man over against him with his sword drawn in his hand: and Joshua went unto him, and said unto him, Art thou for us, or for our adversaries?  And he said, Nay; but as captain of the host of the LORD am I now come. And Joshua fell on his face to the earth, and did worship, and said unto him, What saith my lord unto his servant?  And the captain of the LORD'S host said unto Joshua, Loose thy shoe from off thy foot; for the place whereon thou standest is holy. And Joshua did so.*

God appeared to Joshua right before a great battle. The Captain of the Lord's host reminded this mortal leader that there was One greater who would win the battle for Israel.

This is still true today! Often times, on the eve of some great personal battle, the Lord of hosts will make Himself known to us. As a Christian, we do not have to fight our battles alone!

***Psalm 27:1*** *The LORD is my light and my salvation; whom shall I fear? the LORD is the strength of my life; of whom shall I be afraid?*

***Psalm 35:1-6*** *Plead my cause, O LORD, with them that strive with me: fight against them that fight against me. Take hold of shield and buckler, and stand up for mine help. Draw out also the spear, and stop the way against them that persecute me: say unto my soul, I am thy salvation. Let them be confounded and put to shame that seek after my soul: let them be turned back and brought to confusion that devise my hurt. Let them be as chaff before the wind: and let the angel of the LORD chase them. Let their way be dark and slippery: and let the angel of the LORD persecute them.*

Every teenager will sooner or later have to face his or her Jericho. Remember, you do not have to face it alone!

## 3. A Night Time Voice

***1 Samuel 3:3-10*** *And ere the lamp of God went out in the temple of the LORD, where the ark of God was, and Samuel was laid down to sleep; That the LORD called Samuel: and he answered, Here am I...*
*And the LORD came, and stood, and called as at other times, Samuel, Samuel. Then Samuel answered, Speak; for thy servant heareth.*

Again, as in the case of Moses, God speaks in a special way to a man to call him into special service. It is worthy to note that God called Samuel in his youth. Praise the Lord, God still speaks to young people today.

Also, God came to Samuel in the night hours. God can speak to us at any time, but many times He waits until the world grows quiet. In the night, we still ourselves and because of this, maybe we can finally hear Him.

*Psalm 63:5-6 My soul shall be satisfied as with marrow and fatness; and my mouth shall praise thee with joyful lips: When I remember thee upon my bed, and meditate on thee in the night watches.*

*Psalm 119:55 I have remembered thy name, O LORD, in the night, and have kept thy law.*

*Psalm 119:148 Mine eyes prevent the night watches, that I might meditate in thy word.*

Across America, late at night, God watches and listens for a young man or a young lady who will pray while others sleep. God finds many awake, most playing video games, or watching a Hollywood movie, or, sadly, involved in fleshly sin. But where is the young person who lies awake late at night hungering for the voice of God?

## 4. In a Dream

*1 Kings 3:5 In Gibeon the LORD appeared to Solomon in a dream by night: and God said, Ask what I shall give thee.*

Again, at night, God appears to a young king. He wants to try the heart of Solomon, to see what is most important to him. The Lord gives Solomon one wish, one desire. This young king passes the test by asking God for wisdom.

*1 Kings 3:9 Give therefore thy servant an understanding heart to judge thy people, that I may discern* between good and bad: for who is able to judge this thy so great a people?*

What would your response have been had God made you that offer? God makes Himself known unto the young person who seeks the Lord's wisdom. Have you ever asked God for an understanding heart? For discernment so that you may know what is right and what is wrong? If not, God longs for that!

*James 1:5* If any of you lack wisdom, let him ask of God, that giveth to all men liberally, and upbraideth not; and it shall be given him.

*Proverbs 2:1-6* My son, if thou wilt receive my words, and hide my commandments with thee; So that thou incline thine ear unto wisdom, and apply thine heart to understanding; Yea, if thou criest after knowledge, and liftest up thy voice for understanding; If thou seekest her as silver, and searchest for her as for hid treasures; Then shalt thou understand the fear of the LORD, and find the knowledge of God. For the LORD giveth wisdom: out of his mouth cometh knowledge and understanding.

## 5. A Still Small Voice

*1 Kings 19:9-12* And he came thither unto a cave, and lodged there; and, behold, the word of the LORD came to him, and he said unto him, What doest thou here, Elijah?...And, behold, the LORD passed by, and a great and strong wind rent the mountains, and brake in pieces the rocks before the LORD; but the LORD was not in the wind: and after the wind an earthquake; but the LORD was not in the earthquake: And after the earthquake a fire; but the LORD was not in the fire: and after the fire a still small voice.

Elijah was facing a time of crisis in his ministry as a prophet. He was discouraged to the point where he was praying to die. God fed him, allowed him to rest, and then took Elijah up to the top of Mount Horeb (also called Mount Sinai). God reminded Elijah of His great power by showcasing it in a wind that ripped at the mountain, an earthquake that shook the mountain, and a fire that devoured parts of the mountain. But then, when all grew quiet, God spoke to him in a still small voice.

During times of great discouragement, God often shows Himself to His children. God will do something to remind us of His great power, then speak to us through the still small voice of the Holy Spirit.

Be careful not to grieve the Spirit of God. Be careful not to quench the Spirit of God. It is that still small voice that directs us, teaches us, comforts us, and convicts us. Always be tender and obedient to the voice of God.

## 6. Out of a Whirlwind

*Job 40:6-7 Then answered the LORD unto Job out of the whirlwind, and said, Gird up thy loins now like a man: I will demand of thee, and declare thou unto me.*

Job was a righteous and godly man. He suffered much, and then was accused by his friends of hiding secret sins. These secret sins, they reasoned, were the cause of Job's sufferings.

Job, zealous to defend himself, overstepped the line by declaring himself to be innocent, guiltless and undeserving of God's judgment. Then God showed up to set Job's thinking right.

The lesson we can learn is this: let's be careful that we do not forget that God and God alone is holy and righteous. Sometimes, God has to make an appearance in our lives to put us back in our place. Keep a humble heart, for pride will always produce God's chastening, and humility will always be rewarded with His favor.

*James 4:5-10* *Do ye think that the scripture saith in vain, The spirit that dwelleth in us lusteth to envy? But he giveth more grace. Wherefore he saith, God resisteth the proud, but giveth grace unto the humble... Humble yourselves in the sight of the Lord, and he shall lift you up.*

## 7. In the Fiery Furnace

*Daniel 3:22-25* *Therefore because the king's commandment was urgent, and the furnace exceeding hot, the flame of the fire slew those men that took up Shadrach, Meshach, and Abednego. And these three men, Shadrach, Meshach, and Abednego, fell down bound into the midst of the burning fiery furnace. Then Nebuchadnezzar the king was astonied, and rose up in haste, and spake, and said unto his counsellors, Did not we cast three men bound into the midst of the fire? They answered and said unto the king, True, O king. He answered and said, Lo, I see four men loose, walking in the midst of the fire, and they have no hurt; and the form of the fourth is like the Son of God.*

Three Hebrew children took a stand for God! They refused to bow their knees to a graven image, and because of this, they were thrown into the fiery furnace. But there, they saw the Son of God!

Always stand up for right, no matter the cost. God will always be near the one who refuses to give in to wrong.

There are more than seven Old Testament appearances of God. But from these seven we can learn much about the character of God, and much about His working in our own lives.

## Points to Ponder and Discuss

1. What is the difference between God using a dream in our lives and God appearing to us in a dream to impart some new revelation?

2. Although we know God is always there, at what time or event in your life did you most feel the presence of God?

3. What Old Testament appearance of God can you most relate to?

# -3-
# Seeing Him Who Is Invisible

*Watch the morning watch. Do not see the face of man until you have seen the face of God.* — F. B. Meyer

**Lesson Goals**
1. To understand how God reveals Himself to us today
2. To strengthen our resolve to seek God in His Word
3. To grasp the importance of a transformed life

No Old Testament person ever saw the triune God in all His power, in all His holiness, or in all His glory. Yet God came! They heard His voice, and saw Him in different forms.

What about now, in the church age? How does God choose to reveal Himself to us today?

**How the Invisible God Reveals Himself to Us**

**1. The invisible God is revealed in us.**

*Romans 1:18-19 For the wrath of God is revealed from heaven against all ungodliness and unrighteousness of men, who hold the truth in unrighteousness; Because that which may be known of God is manifest in them...*

Inside of every man, God has placed the knowledge of a Creator. *"...that which may be known of God is manifest in them..."* Down deep in the heart of every man is the knowledge of the existence of Someone mightier than himself. God programmed that knowledge into him. That is why the Bible condemns as foolish a man's declaration of unbelief.

*Psalm 14:1* *The fool hath said in his heart, There is no God...*

## 2. The invisible God is revealed through Creation.

*Romans 1:19-20* *Because that which may be known of God is manifest in them; for God hath showed it unto them. For the invisible things of him from the creation of the world are clearly seen, being understood by the things that are made, even his eternal power and Godhead; so that they are without excuse:*

Creation is a powerful witness as to the existence of a Creator. Everywhere around us is the evidence of intelligent design. These things are "clearly seen" so that unbelievers are "without excuse."

*Psalm 19:1* *The heavens declare the glory of God; and the firmament sheweth his handywork.*

## 3. The invisible God is revealed through the Word of God.

*Romans 10:17* *So then faith cometh by hearing, and hearing by the word of God.*

*Acts 8:35* *Then Philip opened his mouth, and began at the same scripture, and preached unto him Jesus.*

*Hebrews 11:3* *Through faith we understand that the worlds were framed by the word of God, so that things which are seen were not made of things which do appear.*

*2 Timothy 3:15-16* *And that from a child thou hast known the holy scriptures, which are able to make thee wise unto salvation through faith which is in Christ Jesus. All scripture is given by inspiration of God, and is profitable for doctrine, for reproof, for correction, for instruction in righteousness:*

Everything that God wants us to know about Him is revealed to us through His Word. The more you know the Bible, the more you know God. No man can separate the two!  By His Word we understand the character and nature of God.

## 5.  The invisible God is revealed through the working of His Spirit.

*1 Corinthians 2:9-10*    *But as it is written, Eye hath not seen, nor ear heard, neither have entered into the heart of man, the things which God hath prepared for them that love him.  But God hath revealed them unto us by his Spirit: for the Spirit searcheth all things, yea, the deep things of God.*

*John 16:13-15*    *Howbeit when he, the Spirit of truth, is come, he will guide you into all truth: for he shall not speak of himself; but whatsoever he shall hear, that shall he speak: and he will shew you things to come.  He shall glorify me: for he shall receive of mine, and shall shew it unto you.  All things that the Father hath are mine: therefore said I, that he shall take of mine, and shall shew it unto you.*

When Jesus left this earth, He sent the third member of the Godhead to take His place.  The Holy Spirit is sent from the Father to work on the unsaved from the outside, in.   And He works on the believer from the inside, out.  Our invisible God is revealed to us by His Spirit.  The activity of the Holy Spirit in each of our lives is evidence of the existence of God.

## 6.  The invisible God is revealed by the miracle of a transformed life.

*Psalm 40:1-3*    *I waited patiently for the LORD; and he inclined unto me, and heard my cry.  He brought me up also out of an horrible pit, out of the miry clay, and set my feet upon a rock, and established my goings.  And he hath put a new song in my mouth, even praise unto our God: many shall see it, and fear, and shall trust in the LORD.*

God reveals Himself to us through the miracles He performs. We may not see Him, but we can see His transforming power in the lives of people. God changes lives! One of the best ways to show the world that your God exists is by letting God make you into a new creature in Jesus Christ.

**2 Corinthians 5:17** *Therefore if any man be in Christ, he is a new creature: old things are passed away; behold, all things are become new.*

God also performs miracles in response to the prayers of His people. God loves to do the impossible! He likes to remind us often that there are no limits to His power. These special miracles increase our faith, and confirm in our hearts the existence of God.

Every day, in a multitude of ways, our invisible God can be seen! Inside of each of us His existence is manifested. Creation gives testimony to God. Through His Word, through His Spirit, and through His transforming power, mankind is given all the evidence that he needs to KNOW that there is a God. God still insists that faith be involved. Only a fool would look around and say, "There is no God."

## Points to Ponder and Discuss

1. Atheists have an opinion of God. God also has an opinion of the atheist. What is that opinion? Why?

2. Name one character trait of God, taught to us in His Word. In what Bible story do we see this character trait exhibited?

3. Remember back to an instance when the Holy Spirit revealed to you His presence. How did that occur?

# -4-
# Our Invisible Savior

*I trust I feel something of that hidden, but powerful presence of Christ, whilst I am preaching to you.*
*— George Whitefield*

**Lesson Goals**
1. To better understand why faith is necessary for salvation
2. To understand how to build a love relationship with our Savior, even though we have never seen Him
3. To understand that we will one day see Jesus, and to learn how not to be ashamed on that day

**Building a Relationship with our Invisible Redeemer**

**1. To become a Christian, you must put your heart belief in a Savior you have never seen.**

Just as belief in God the Father requires faith, salvation through Jesus Christ is only available by faith.

***Romans 5:1-2**, Therefore being justified by faith, we have peace with God through our Lord Jesus Christ: By whom also we have access by faith into this grace wherein we stand, and rejoice in hope of the glory of God.*

***Ephesians 2:8-9**, For by grace are ye saved through faith; and that not of yourselves: it is the gift of God: Not of works, lest any man should boast.*

When God created mankind, He placed within us the capacity for faith. As an act of our free will, each of us can choose to believe in something that we have never seen.

Salvation of a man's soul requires an exercise of faith. To be saved you must, by faith, believe the Gospel of Jesus Christ. You must choose to believe that He died on the cross for your sins as the Scripture describes. You must, by faith, believe in His burial and resurrection from the dead. You must accept that He did this for you, and that there is no other way to Heaven except through Jesus Christ and His finished work.

You were not there at Calvary to see Him die. No, you were not there three days later when the stone was rolled away and He walked out alive. If you choose to believe these things happened, you must choose to believe them by faith.

*Galatians 3:26, For ye are all the children of God by faith in Christ Jesus.*

**2. As a Christian, you will grow to love a Savior you have never seen.**

*1 Peter 1:7-8, That the trial of your faith, being much more precious than of gold that perisheth, though it be tried with fire, might be found unto praise and honour and glory at the appearing of Jesus Christ: Whom having not seen, ye love; in whom, though now ye see him not, yet believing, ye rejoice with joy unspeakable and full of glory:*

What a statement! *"Whom having not seen, ye love..."* At first, that seems impossible. How can you love someone you have never physically met?

Ask a mother who has yet to hold her unborn child, but from the moment she finds out she is pregnant, she loves him.

Ask the grandparents, who receive word that their daughter has delivered their granddaughter, yet live far away and have not yet seen that child. Ask them if they love that little girl.

As the West was settled, in the early days of our nation's history, many men courted women from the East through letters. Often, they would not meet their wife-to-be until she arrived on a stage coach. Both would see each other for the first time, yet already be in love. Some of these couples married within days of that meeting.

Yes, God has given us the capacity to love someone we have never met. He has also given us a love letter from our Savior — the King James Bible. Jesus proved His love for us by dying on the cross for our sins. Although we have never seen Him with our human eyes, we have heard His voice through the pages of Scripture. We have talked with Him through the vehicle of prayer. And we have felt His love, His comfort and His guidance through the working of His Spirit in our lives.

Christians throughout the New Testament age share this testimony: "Yes, I love Jesus. And no, I have never seen Him."

### 3. As you become a disciple, you give your life to serve a Savior you have never seen.

To someone who has never been born again, this may seem odd. To the atheist and agnostic, this seems crazy. Yet, in every generation, there are millions of redeemed saints who have sacrificed their time, their wealth, their personal ambitions and — for some — their very lives for Jesus Christ their Lord.

In the Gospels, we read of fishermen who forsook the family business to follow Jesus. A tax collector resigned and walked away from his lucrative practice to be a full-time disciple. In the book of the Acts of the Apostles, we see people from all walks of life — soldiers, merchants, politicians, and common laborers — who counted it the greatest joy to give up everything to

31

be a disciple of Jesus Christ. Most of these new converts had never actually met the Lord Jesus Christ. They became disciples to a Savior they had never seen.

Over 2000 years of church history contain thousands of stories of men and women who gave up all to serve their invisible Lord. Many walked away from earthly fame and fortune.

*Billy Sunday* walked away from a professional baseball career after receiving Jesus Christ as his Savior. The remainder of his life was spent in evangelism.

*Bobby Bonner* also chose to retire early from professional baseball to become a missionary to Zambia. He served there for 26 years, reaching people for Jesus Christ.

*Evangelist Joe Boyd* was the first-round draft pick of the Washington Redskins, yet turned it down to give his life to preach the Gospel.

*Pastor Mike Holloway* was a Navy fighter pilot but refused reenlistment after being called to preach. He has pastored in Kokomo, Indiana for decades.

*Bill Borden* (1887-1913), heir to the Borden family fortune, received from his parents a trip around the world for his high school graduation present. The then 16 year old young man was burdened for the unreached multitudes as he traveled through Asia, the Middle East and Europe. Bill came home determined to give his life on the mission field.

Bill gave away much of his wealth, attended seminary at Princeton, and from there, he sailed toward China. He had a desire to reach Muslims for the Lord Jesus Christ, so he stopped in Egypt to study Arabic. While there, he contracted spinal meningitis. Sadly, within a month, 25-year-old William Borden was dead.

Later, these three phrases were found written in his Bible: *No reserves, No retreats, No regrets.* He did these things for a Savior he had never met.

***C. T. Studd***, a professional cricket player, quit the sport to become a missionary to China. Upon receiving a large inheritance at 25 years of age, he gave it all away to the Lord's work. In a letter home, written near the end of his life, he penned these words:

*"As I believe I am now nearing my departure from this world, I have but a few things to rejoice in; they are these:*

*1. That God called me to China and I went in spite of utmost opposition from all my loved ones.*

*2. That I joyfully acted as Christ told that rich young man to act.*

*3. That I deliberately at the call of God, when alone on the Bibby liner in 1910, gave up my life for this work, which was to be henceforth not for the Sudan only, but for the whole unevangelized World.*

*My only joys therefore are that when God has given me a work to do, I have not refused it."*

**4. As you serve your invisible Savior, He rewards you with great joy and a touch of glory.**

Why have so many been willing to sacrifice so much to serve our invisible Savior? Is there a reward so wonderfully rare that it makes a life of sacrifice worth it?

*1 Peter 1:8, Whom having not seen, ye love; in whom, though now ye see him not, yet believing, ye rejoice with joy unspeakable and full of glory:*

The immediate reward is the joy and glory we experience by leading others to the Lord. The afore mentioned C. T. Studd, upon winning his first soul to the Lord, wrote:

*"I cannot tell you what joy it gave me to bring the first soul to the Lord Jesus Christ. I have tasted almost all the pleasures that this world can give ... but those*

*pleasures were as nothing compared to the joy that the saving of that one soul gave me."*

The eternal reward will be the opportunity to one day look into the face of the One we have loved and served, but never seen. To hear our Savior say, "Well done, thou good and faithful servant."

Every Christian has an appointment at the judgment seat of Christ. There we will receive reward for our service, or suffer loss of reward because of our selfishness and slothfulness. What will that day be like for you?

***Mark 8:38****, Whosoever therefore shall be ashamed of me and of my words in this adulterous and sinful generation; of him also shall the Son of man be ashamed, when he cometh in the glory of his Father with the holy angels.*

## Points to Ponder and Discuss

1. Are you saved? If asked, could you and would you publicly give your salvation testimony?

2. What is the greatest thing you have ever sacrificed for your invisible Savior?

3. If you were to stand before Jesus Christ today to answer for how you have thus far spent your life, what would His response be to your report?

# -5-
# Our Invisible Companion

*Breathe in me, O Holy Spirit, that my thoughts*
*may all be holy.* — *Augustine*

**Lesson Goals**
1. To be introduced to the third person of the Trinity, the Holy Spirit of God
2. To better understand the Holy Spirit's workings in our lives
3. To examine and, if necessary, repair our personal relationship with the Holy Spirit

## Who is the Holy Spirit?

The Holy Spirit is God.  He is also invisible. The Holy Spirit is as much God as God the Father and God the Son.  Altogether, God the Father, God the Son, and God the Holy Spirit make up the Trinity.

***John 3:8,*** *The wind bloweth where it listeth, and thou hearest the sound thereof, but canst not tell whence it cometh, and whither it goeth: so is every one that is born of the Spirit.*

## Understanding the Trinity

The Bible declares God to be one God.  Yet He chooses to reveal Himself to us in three distinct personalities:  God the Father, God the Son, and God the Spirit.

How can God be one and three at the same time? Several illustrations have been used to help us grasp the concept of the Trinity. A rope, if examined, is not just one rope, but three smaller ropes intertwined to make one.

The atomic make up of water remains the same, yet it can take three distinct and different forms: liquid, solid (ice), and vapor (steam). All three different, yet all still one.

Although these earthly illustrations may help us somewhat, the truth is that it is impossible for mere mortals to mentally grasp our infinite and eternal God. God cannot and will not be reduced to a scientific formula or a test tube experiment. He is to be accepted and believed by faith, not dissected or deduced by intellect. No man can ever truly understand the greatness and uniqueness of the Trinity.

*Isaiah 55:8-9, For my thoughts are not your thoughts, neither are your ways my ways, saith the LORD. For as the heavens are higher than the earth, so are my ways higher than your ways, and my thoughts than your thoughts.*

## The Holy Spirit's Work Amongst the Unsaved

Before Jesus died on the cross, He explained to His disciples that He must leave them. But He also promised to send Another to continue His work in them and amongst them.

*John 14:16-17, And I will pray the Father, and he shall give you another Comforter, that he may abide with you for ever; Even the Spirit of truth; whom the world cannot receive, because it seeth him not, neither knoweth him: but ye know him; for he dwelleth with you, and shall be in you.*

The Holy Spirit was sent to assist the disciples by empowering the Gospel to bring conviction of sin to the hearts of those who were lost.

*John 16:7-8, Nevertheless I tell you the truth; It is expedient for you that I go away: for if I go not away, the Comforter will not come unto you; but if I depart, I will send him unto you. And when he is come, he will reprove the world of sin, and of righteousness, and of judgment:*

There are three things that the Holy Spirit does to convict a person of their need of a Savior.

**1. Reproves the sinfulness of man.** The Holy Spirit uses the preaching of the Word to reprove our hearts concerning our own sinfulness. No man has ever perfectly kept the commands of God as found in the Bible. The Spirit brings conviction upon us for our disobedience to the Word of God.

**2. Reveals the righteousness of God.** The Bible also reveals to us the holiness of God. When our sinfulness is compared to God's holiness, the Spirit again brings conviction and fear to our hearts. He convinces us that no man can stand before a holy God and be accepted on his own merit.

**3. Warns us of the judgment that awaits.** The Holy Spirit then uses the Bible doctrines connected with judgment to warn the sinner of the eternal consequences of rejecting Christ as Savior.

*Romans 5:12, Wherefore, as by one man sin entered into the world, and death by sin; and so death passed upon all men, for that all have sinned:*

*Revelation 20:14-15, And death and hell were cast into the lake of fire. This is the second death. And whosoever was not found written in the book of life was cast into the lake of fire.*

The Holy Spirit prepares the heart of a lost man to be willing to consider and accept the grace and mercy of

God. No man has ever gotten saved who did not first become convinced that he was lost. No man has ever been converted without first becoming convicted — no conviction, no conversion.

**4. Urges us to "Come!"** There is a wonderful fourth work of the Spirit in relationship to the lost. Once He has convinced a man of his need of a Savior, He then urges that man to come to the Savior.

*Revelation 22:17, And the Spirit and the bride say, Come. And let him that heareth say, Come. And let him that is athirst come. And whosoever will, let him take the water of life freely.*

What a wonderful thing when a man, woman or child comes under Holy Spirit conviction, understands the gospel story, and decides to come to Jesus and receive His free gift of forgiveness and eternal life! As you can see, the Holy Spirit plays a big part in our salvation. And He is still working on lost sinners today.

## The Holy Spirit's Work in the Life of the Believer

Once a person is saved, the Holy Spirit begins a new phase of ministry in his or her life.

**1. The Holy Spirit indwells the believer.** The moment you receive Jesus as your Savior, the Holy Spirit comes to indwell you. He literally takes up residence in your body. Your body becomes His home.

*1 Corinthians 6:19-20, What? know ye not that your body is the temple of the Holy Ghost which is in you, which ye have of God, and ye are not your own? For ye are bought with a price: therefore glorify God in your body, and in your spirit, which are God's.*

*2 Corinthians 1:21-22, Now he which stablisheth us with you in Christ, and hath anointed us, is God;*

*Who hath also sealed us, and given the earnest of the Spirit in our hearts.*

**2. The Holy Spirit tutors us as we study God's Word.** The Holy Spirit was the One who empowered men to write the inspired Words of God. He also is the One who will open our understanding to the hidden truths of the Scriptures.

*1 Corinthians 2:12-14, Now we have received, not the spirit of the world, but the spirit which is of God; that we might know the things that are freely given to us of God. Which things also we speak, not in the words which man's wisdom teacheth, but which the Holy Ghost teacheth; comparing spiritual things with spiritual. But the natural man receiveth not the things of the Spirit of God: for they are foolishness unto him: neither can he know them, because they are spiritually discerned.*

**3. The Holy Spirit assists us as we pray.** At times, we don't even know what to pray! During those times, the Spirit of God speaks to the Father for us.

*Romans 8:26-27, Likewise the Spirit also helpeth our infirmities: for we know not what we should pray for as we ought: but the Spirit itself maketh intercession for us with groanings which cannot be uttered. And he that searcheth the hearts knoweth what is the mind of the Spirit, because he maketh intercession for the saints according to the will of God.*

**4. The Holy Spirit comforts us during difficult times.** Jesus promised us a Comforter! How many times is our sorrow so great, that we don't know how we will get through the day? Yet the Spirit sustains us.

*John 14:16, And I will pray the Father, and he shall give you another Comforter, that he may abide with you for ever.*

**5. The Holy Spirit directs us to divine appointments.** As we already learned, it is the Spirit's mission to prepare the lost to receive the Gospel. But He also works in the life of Spirit-filled Christians to direct them to those who are ready to be saved.

*Acts 8:29-30, Then the Spirit said unto Philip, Go near, and join thyself to this chariot. And Philip ran thither to him, and heard him read the prophet Esaias, and said, Understandest thou what thou readest?*

**6. The Holy Spirit empowers us as we witness for Christ. He enables us to win the lost!**

*Acts 1:8, But ye shall receive power, after that the Holy Ghost is come upon you: and ye shall be witnesses unto me both in Jerusalem, and in all Judaea, and in Samaria, and unto the uttermost part of the earth.*

**7. The Holy Spirit convicts us when we sin.** Always be tender to the working of the Spirit in your own life. He convicts us to keep us clean and usable.

*1 Thessalonians 5:19, Quench not the Spirit.*

All of these things are performed by our Invisible Companion. Like the wind, He is not seen, but the effects of His moving are evident all around us.

**Points to Ponder and Discuss**

1. Remember what it was like when God's Spirit was preparing you to be saved? Try to put it into words.

2. How would you describe your relationship with the Holy Spirit right now?

3. Is it OK to pray to the Holy Spirit?

# -6-
# Our Invisible Helpers (Part 1)

*The biggest answers to our prayers are in the realm of the unseen.* — Oswald Chambers

**Lesson Goals**
1. To biblically define and describe the angels of God
2. To understand how they minister today
3. To be challenged by their loyalty and dedication to God

    A study of God's angels is certainly worthwhile. Angels are created beings, dedicated to serving their Creator. They are never to be worshipped, and should be viewed in their proper place — as messengers and servants of God.
    *Colossians 2:18, Let no man beguile you of your reward in a voluntary humility and worshipping of angels, intruding into those things which he hath not seen, vainly puffed up by his fleshly mind,*
    *Revelation 19:10, And I fell at his feet to worship him. And he said unto me, See thou do it not: I am thy fellowservant, and of thy brethren that have the testimony of Jesus: worship God: for the testimony of Jesus is the spirit of prophecy.*

## *10 Things You Should Know About the Angels of God*

## 1. Angels are ministering spirits who obediently serve their Lord.
    The word *angel* means *messenger*. They excel in strength. Their loyalty to God is without question. An-

gels obey the Lord's commands and hearken unto His voice. They are God's ministers who do His pleasure.

*Psalm 103:19-21    The LORD hath prepared his throne in the heavens; and his kingdom ruleth over all. Bless the LORD, ye his angels, that excel in strength, that do his commandments, hearkening unto the voice of his word.  Bless ye the LORD, all ye his hosts; ye ministers of his, that do his pleasure.*

## 2.   Angels are spirits, but power is given to them to become visible in the semblance of human form.

*Psalm 104:4    Who maketh his angels spirits; his ministers a flaming fire:*

*Genesis 19:1-5    And there came two angels to Sodom at even; and Lot sat in the gate of Sodom: and Lot seeing them rose up to meet them... And they called unto Lot, and said unto him, Where are the men which came in to thee this night?*

*Judges 13:6    Then the woman came and told her husband, saying, A man of God came unto me, and his countenance was like the countenance of an angel of God, very terrible: but I asked him not whence he was, neither told he me his name:*

*Acts 12:6-7    And when Herod would have brought him forth, the same night Peter was sleeping between two soldiers, bound with two chains: and the keepers before the door kept the prison.  And, behold, the angel of the Lord came upon him, and a light shined in the prison: and he smote Peter on the side, and raised him up, saying, Arise up quickly. And his chains fell off from his hands.*

*Hebrews 13:2    Be not forgetful to entertain strangers: for thereby some have entertained angels unawares.*

Throughout history, God has, at times, sent His angels to Earth to deliver messages to men.   Many times, they took on the form of men. Although angels are spirits, God allows them to sometimes appear to man as men. Although this is not as common today, the Bible does remind us to be hospitable and helpful to strangers. We are reminded that some who did so in the Old Testament did not realize that they were entertaining angels.

### 3. "Angel" is used in the masculine gender, though in a human, physical sense, they are genderless.

*Matthew 22:29-30 Jesus answered and said unto them, Ye do err, not knowing the scriptures, nor the power of God. For in the resurrection they neither marry, nor are given in marriage, but are as the angels of God in heaven.*

Angels are always identified as men, and the original word is always in the masculine form. However, Jesus made it plain that the angels do not marry. They are created beings who appear as men, but who were not created to reproduce.

### 4. Angels are extremely numerous.

*Matthew 26:53 Thinkest thou that I cannot now pray to my Father, and he shall presently give me more than twelve legions of angels?*

*Hebrews 12:22 But ye are come unto mount Sion, and unto the city of the living God, the heavenly Jerusalem, and to an innumerable company of angels,*

What is the largest gathering of people you have ever personally seen or been a part of? Did you attempt to estimate the crowd? Was it impossible?

God uses the word "innumerable" when describing the company of angels. What a sight that will be when we get to Heaven!

### 5. Angels have a unique relationship to the believers.

Angels are ministering spirits, sent to minister to us who are heirs of salvation. This ministry provides us with physical safety and personal well-being. Angels are our heavenly body guards, God's security team for the saved.

*1 Kings 19:5-7   And as he (Elijah) lay and slept under a juniper tree, behold, then an angel touched him, and said unto him, Arise and eat. And he looked, and, behold, there was a cake baken on the coals, and a cruse of water at his head. And he did eat and drink, and laid him down again...*

*Psalm 34:7   The angel of the LORD encampeth round about them that fear him, and delivereth them.*

*Daniel 6:22   My God hath sent his angel, and hath shut the lions' mouths, that they have not hurt me...*

*Acts 5:19   But the angel of the Lord by night opened the prison doors, and brought them forth...*

*Hebrews 1:14   Are they not all ministering spirits, sent forth to minister for them who shall be heirs of salvation?*

There is great comfort in knowing that God dispatches His army of protecting servants on our behalf.


## Points to Ponder and Discuss

1. Name a character trait of angels that we should emulate.

2. Can you name any Bible angels?

3. Should an angel of God ever request or accept worship? Why not?

# Our Invisible Helpers (Part 2)

*The angel fetched Peter out of prison, but it was prayer that fetched the angel. — Thomas Watson*

**Lesson Goals**
1. Review the first five truths about angels from the last lesson.
2. To further understand the ministry of angels in our lives
3. To understand the future work of angels in the end times

### *10 Things You Should Know About the Angels of God (continued)*

**6. Angels have a special responsibility to children.**
    *Matthew 18:10    Take heed that ye despise not one of these little ones; for I say unto you, That in heaven their angels do always behold the face of my Father which is in heaven.*

    *Psalm 91:11    For he shall give his angels charge over thee, to keep thee in all thy ways.*

    Jesus loves the little children! And He assigns His angels to watch over them. All of us can think back over our childhood to times when we could have been seriously injured or even killed. How many times do God's assigned protectors step in and spare one of His little ones?

**7. Angels observe us.**
    *1 Corinthians 4:9    For I think that God hath set*

*forth us the apostles last, as it were appointed to death: for we are made a spectacle unto the world, and to angels, and to men.*

This fact should motivate us as Christians! Angels are a part of that great "cloud of witnesses" who are rooting for us to live for God. They respond with great joy at the salvation of a soul.

***Luke 15:10*** *Likewise, I say unto you, there is joy in the presence of the angels of God over one sinner that repenteth.*

When was the last time God used you to ignite a celebration in Heaven? We should be always looking for opportunities to share the Gospel with the lost. I wonder if the angels of God are puzzled over many Christians' lack of concern for those without Christ?

## 8. Angels receive departing saints.

***Luke 16:22*** *And it came to pass, that the beggar died, and was carried by the angels into Abraham's bosom: the rich man also died, and was buried;*

How comforting to know that God sends His angels to accompany the souls of men from Earth to Heaven. Death is a scary thing! But the first things we will see are our kind, comforting, heavenly companions.

Many Christians have shared testimony to what they saw in the faces and in the actions of dying Christian loved ones. Often, the departing one appears to see things that the rest of us cannot. Many have spoken last words that make us wonder at the invisible creation that they, for the first time, can see.

In a book entitled *Death-Bed Scenes*, first published in 1851, Dr. Davis W. Clark collected eye-witness accounts of the last words and testimonies of both dying saints and sinners alike. Here is a sampling of some accounts found in this book.

# Dying Words of Saints

**Dr. Philip Doddridge** (died 1751) was a preacher of the Gospel, yet took ill and soon lingered near death. He told his wife, "I cannot express to you what a morning I have had; such delightful and transporting view of the heavenly world is my Father now indulging me with, as no words can express." He passed shortly after.

**John Holland's** (died 1809) family recorded the last words of this faithful Christian layman.

"What brightness is this I see? Have you lighted up my candles?"

His son answered, "No, it is the sunshine."

"Sunshine?" John smiled then answered, "Nay, my Savior's shine. Now farewell, world; welcome Heaven! ...I feel His mercy; I see His majesty: whether in body or out of body I cannot tell — God knoweth; but I see things that are unutterable."

**Lady Elizabeth Hastings** (died 1740) passed away after battling cancer. Her last words, "Lord, what is it that I see? O the greatness of the glory that is revealed in me! That is before me!"

**Mrs. Elizabeth James** (died 1856) went to Heaven with these words for her friend, "How beautiful will you be when you come thither! You will not know yourself — your clothes will be changed!" Then to Jesus, "Open, Lord; I can stay no longer. My dear Redeemer! My dear Redeemer!" Soon after, she fell asleep.

**Mary Frances Wright** (died 1850), an eight year old girl who loved church and loved the Savior, fell gravely ill. She spoke to her mother on her death bed, "You have been a kind mother to me." She also spoke of her father, who had died the year before, requesting to be buried beside him. "I shall be with him in Heaven."

Her last words, "I see Heaven, and the angels are round about the room." Her mother then asked whether she would rather die or live.

"I would rather die and go home to Heaven." She then departed this world, accompanied by the angels.

## Dying Words of Sinners

It would be wrong to leave this subject without reminding all of us that not everyone who dies has accepted Jesus as Savior. As precious as the death of a saint, nothing is more horrid than a soul departing without Christ.

**Voltaire,** the self-proclaimed infidel cried out to his doctor as he died, "I am abandoned by God and man!" He then said, "I will give you half of what I am worth, if you can give me six months of life!"

The doctor answered, "I cannot give you six weeks," to which Voltaire replied, "Then I shall go to Hell, and you will go with me!" Soon after, he expired.

**Louisa** was the name Rev. Jacob Abbott called her in his written testimony. He named her thus to protect the feelings of her family. He described her as a "young lady whose blooming countenance and cheerful air showed perfect health and high elation of spirits." But she had little interest in the things of the Lord. Her explanation, "I wish to live a gay and merry life 'til just before my death, and then to become pious and die happy."

Rev. Abbott invited a few of the young ladies of society to meet at his house, and Louisa came along. He urged them in the matter of salvation, and Louisa was "evidently moved, but endeavored to hide her feelings." He asked them to return in a week's time, and at that meeting had this personal conversation with Louisa.

"Louisa, have you been long thinking about the subject of religion?"

"I always thought the subject important, sir. But have not attended to it as I suppose I ought."

"Do you now feel the subject more important than you have previously?"

"I don't know, sir. I want to be a Christian."

"Do you feel that you are a sinner, Louisa?"

She replied, "I know I am a sinner, for the Bible says so; but I suppose I do not feel it enough."

A week later he met with her again, and the conversation picked up where it had left off.

"Well Louisa, now count the cost. Are you ready to give up all for Christ?"

Although under deep conviction, she answered, "I am afraid not."

She came back for the next two weeks, but her concern for her soul seemed to have diminished as she was caught up in society life and popularity of the world.

Three months later, Rev. Abbott received word that she was deathly ill and asking for him. As he walked into her sick chamber, she cried out, "I am sick and may die. I know I am not a Christian, and O! If I die in this state, what will become of me?"

He spent the next several days visiting her and imploring her to receive Christ. Her answer, "O, sir, I know the Savior is merciful, but somehow I cannot go to Him. I know not why. O, I am miserable indeed."

He then opened the Bible and read to her.

"O sir, none of these promises are for me! I find no peace for my troubled soul. I have long been sinning against God, and know He is summoning me to render up my account!"

The next day, her last day, and her answer to salvation was this, "I know God is ready to forgive the sincerely penitent; but my sorrow is not sorrow for sin, but of its awful penalty."

Later that afternoon he called again. This is what he later penned:

"Every eye in the room was filled with tears, but poor Louisa saw not, and heeded not their weeping. Her reason was gone... I can still see now her restless form, her swollen veins, the hectic, burning cheeks, the eyes rolling wildly around the room, and the weeping friends." In that state, she died.

*Isaiah 55:6 Seek ye the LORD while he may be found, call ye upon him while he is near:*

What a contrast between the dying saint and the dying sinner! If you are unsaved, be saved today. You do not want to face a Christ-less eternity!

## 9. Angels will accompany Christ when He comes to Earth to set up His kingdom.

*Matthew 25:31 When the Son of man shall come in his glory, and all the holy angels with him, then shall he sit upon the throne of his glory:*

Angels will accompany Christ when He returns to the earth in glory, and will assist Christ during His millennial reign. We are also blessed to rule and reign with Christ for this 1,000 year period.

## 10. Angels will assist at the judgment seat.

*Matthew 13:40-42 As therefore the tares are gathered and burned in the fire; so shall it be in the end of this world. The Son of man shall send forth his angels, and they shall gather out of his kingdom all things that offend, and them which do iniquity; And shall cast them into a furnace of fire: there shall be wailing and gnashing of teeth.*

Angels will be involved in sending those who rejected Christ into eternal punishment.

Angels are God's amazing servants; unique, powerful, loyal, and dedicated! One day, Heaven will reveal how often God's children were assisted, protected and strengthened by angels.

## Points to Ponder

1. Why does God have angels present at the death of a saint?

2. Is there a story in your family about an unusual death bed experience? Ask your parents and grandparents.

3. Imagine God's strong angels capturing and casting the lost into the Lake of Fire! What a horrific scene to ponder.

# -8-
# Satan, Our Invisible Enemy (Part 1)

*All Satan's apples have worms.* —John R. Rice

**Lesson Goals**
1. To better understand the diabolical nature of Satan
2. To better understand his methods of attack
3. To insulate ourselves from his deceitfulness

The next two lessons are about our invisible enemy, the Devil. He is real, and should never be underestimated. However, we can rejoice that *"greater is He that is in me, than he that is in the world."*

## 5 Things Every Teenager Needs to Know About the Devil

### 1. Satan is real.
*Isaiah 14:9-17   How art thou fallen from heaven, O Lucifer, son of the morning! how art thou cut down to the ground, which didst weaken the nations!   For thou hast said in thine heart, I will ascend into heaven, I will exalt my throne above the stars of God: I will sit also upon the mount of the congregation, in the sides of the north:   I will ascend above the heights of the clouds; I will be like the most High.   Yet thou shalt be brought down to hell, to the sides of the pit...*

In eternity past, Satan existed as Lucifer, one of three of God's high archangels (Michael and Gabriel, the other two). He had beauty, power, position, and a following. He was a musical being, blessed with divine talent and a divine appointment where he exercised that talent.  He lived in the presence of God, wanted for nothing, existed in peace, surrounded by perfection and piety.  Lucifer had everything but one thing, and that was worship!  He longed to be "like the most High."  The desire to be worshipped drove him to rebellion, drove him to deception, and eventually drove him out of Heaven.  God shares His worship with no one.

Satan desires to be worshipped.  He craves it, he longs for it, he glories in it, he fights for it, he will kill for it.  In pagan lands, he has found worship.  In pagan religion, he has enjoyed adoration.  In pagan cultures, Satan has received what he longed for.  He goes by different names: Beelzebub, The Pythian's Apollo, Belial, Asmodeus, Meresin, Abaddon, Diabolus, Mammon, Astema, Azazel, and Sama-el.

In the Bible he is called Abaddon, the Accuser, Adversary, Angel of the bottomless pit, Angel of light, Belial, Devil, dragon, enemy, father of lies, god of this world, great dragon, liar, Lucifer, man of sin, murderer, old serpent, power of darkness, prince of this world, prince of the air, prince of darkness, roaring lion, ruler of darkness, Satan, serpent, tempter, thief, wicked one.  To him, it matters not what you call him, as long as you worship him instead of Jehovah God.

## 2.  Satan is a deceiver.

*Genesis 3:1-7   Now the serpent was more subtil than any beast of the field which the LORD God had made. And he said unto the woman, Yea, hath God said, Ye shall not eat of every tree of the garden?*

Satan makes his first appearance in the Bible in the third chapter of Genesis.  He confronts Eve and deceives her.  His tactics have not changed, so we would do well to study them.

a)  **Satan deceives Eve into questioning the**

**words of God.** *"Yea, hath God said...?"* Satan always tries to get men to question the words of God. "Did God really mean that?" "Is that what He really said?" Satan still does that today! He wants to get you to question the Scriptures instead of just accepting what they say.

b) **Satan lies to Eve.** *"Ye shall not surely die."* God said that she would, Satan says that she wouldn't. God warns us that Satan is a liar, but Satan wants us to believe God is a liar. Someone is lying to Eve!

*Hebrews 6:18 That by two immutable things, in which it was impossible for God to lie, we might have a strong consolation, who have fled for refuge to lay hold upon the hope set before us:*

*John 8:44 Ye are of your father the devil, and the lusts of your father ye will do. He was a murderer from the beginning, and abode not in the truth, because there is no truth in him. When he speaketh a lie, he speaketh of his own: for he is a liar, and the father of it.*

Never trust the Devil! It is impossible for God to lie, and it is impossible for the Devil to tell the truth.

c) **Satan deceives Eve into believing that God is withholding something from her.** *"For God doth know that in the day ye eat thereof, then your eyes shall be opened..."* The Devil is trying to convince Eve that God is robbing her of something – that she is missing out. Satan is telling Eve that God's rule against eating the fruit is unfair and selfish on God's part.

This still works today! Satan convinces young people that authority is against them and rules are robbing them of good things. And sadly, young people are falling for his lie.

d) **Satan deceives Eve into believing that she,**

not God, should be able to decide what is good and what is evil. *"...and ye shall be as gods, knowing good and evil."* Satan is telling her, "You can be a god. You can know or decide what is good or evil."

Sound familiar? Ever have these thoughts? "I should be able to decide what is right and wrong for myself." That was not your thought! That was Satan whispering in your ear.

e) **Satan deceives Eve into closely examining what was forbidden, and into trying it for herself.** *"And when the woman saw that the tree was good for food, and that it was pleasant to the eyes, and a tree to be desired to make one wise...."* God tells us to flee temptation; Satan tells us to court it.

f) **Satan deceives Eve into offering what was forbidden to another.** *"...she took of the fruit thereof, and did eat, and gave also unto her husband with her; and he did eat."* The wicked part of Satan's plan is that he is not just interested in causing you to fall, he is just as interested in enlisting you to cause others to fall. The master deceiver is great at this. Unfortunately, guilt likes company. His best recruiters are former victims.

Satan has deceived some of God's choicest servants! Entire nations have been deceived by him. Be wise, and be careful!

***Revelation 20:10*** *And the devil that deceived them was cast into the lake of fire and brimstone...*

## Points to Ponder and Discuss
1. Think about this thought: "Pride has turned angels into devils." How is this true?

2. Name ways the Devil is tricking people today.

# Satan, Our Invisible Enemy (Part 2)

*Hell is the highest reward that the Devil can offer you for being a servant of his. — Billy Sunday*

## Lesson Goals
1. Review the first two truths about the Devil from our last lesson.
2. To learn how we can defeat the devil
3. To learn how the devil will forever be defeated

### *5 Things Every Teenager Needs to Know About the Devil (continued)*

## 3. Satan is angry and desperate.

*Revelation 12:12 Therefore rejoice, ye heavens, and ye that dwell in them. Woe to the inhabiters of the earth and of the sea! for the devil is come down unto you, having great wrath, because he knoweth that he hath but a short time.*

The Devil is a defeated foe. He is under no illusion that he can defeat the Lord. Because of that, he is angry and he is desperate. The Devil never rests! He works 24/7 to destroy people. This makes Satan a dangerous foe.

*1 Peter 5:8 Be sober, be vigilant; because your adversary the devil, as a roaring lion, walketh about, seeking whom he may devour:*

The Devil knows that his time is short. And he is determined to destroy as many people as he can during the short time he has left.

## 4. Satan is beatable.

*Revelation 12:9-11    And the great dragon was cast out, that old serpent, called the Devil, and Satan, which deceiveth the whole world: he was cast out into the earth, and his angels were cast out with him.  And I heard a loud voice saying in heaven, Now is come salvation, and strength, and the kingdom of our God, and the power of his Christ: for the accuser of our brethren is cast down, which accused them before our God day and night.  And they overcame him by the blood of the Lamb, and by the word of their testimony; and they loved not their lives unto the death.*

Satan is beatable!  Remember, he is a defeated foe.  Never forget what I will say next:  THE DEVIL CANNOT WIN A VICTORY AGAINST US UNLESS WE HAND IT TO HIM!

So how can we overcome our invisible enemy?

a) **You can overcome Satan by the blood of the Lamb.**  There is power in the name of Jesus.  There is power in the blood!  Anytime you are under a satanic assault, always invoke the name of Christ and plead the blood.  Resist the Devil and he will flee from you.

b) **You can overcome Satan by the word of your testimony.**  Every satanic assault should be answered with a counter-attack.   There is amazing power in your personal testimony.  During times of intense temptation, intensify your soul winning efforts.  Share your salvation testimony with as many people as you can, and you will overcome the Devil.

c) **You can overcome Satan with a martyr's mentality.**  The worst the Devil can threaten you with is Heaven!  If you grow to the point where living for God is more important to you than life itself, you become unbeatable! A willingness to die for the Lord also gives you the ability to live for the Lord.

*Matthew 10:28    And fear not them which kill the body, but are not able to kill the soul: but rather fear him which is able to destroy both soul and body in hell.*

*Philippians 1:20-21    According to my earnest expectation and my hope, that in nothing I shall be ashamed, but that with all boldness, as always, so now also Christ shall be magnified in my body, whether it be by life, or by death.  For to me to live is Christ, and to die is gain.*

## 5.  Satan is doomed.

*Revelation 20:7-10    And when the thousand years are expired, Satan shall be loosed out of his prison,  And shall go out to deceive the nations which are in the four quarters of the earth, Gog and Magog, to gather them together to battle: the number of whom is as the sand of the sea.  And they went up on the breadth of the earth, and compassed the camp of the saints about, and the beloved city: and fire came down from God out of heaven, and devoured them.  And the devil that deceived them was cast into the lake of fire and brimstone, where the beast and the false prophet are, and shall be tormented day and night for ever and ever.*

Never forget, in the end, the Lord Jesus will reign triumphant upon the throne for all eternity, and the Devil will be tormented in the Lake of Fire for all eternity.  If you are a Christian, you are on the winning side.

Don't spend your life serving a doomed, deceitful, unemployed archangel!  In the end, we will all wonder at why we allowed him the victories that he achieved.  Notice the disdain that will be heaped upon him in the end:

*Isaiah 14:12-19    How art thou fallen from heaven, O Lucifer, son of the morning! how art thou cut down to the ground, which didst weaken the nations! For thou hast said in thine heart, I will ascend into heaven, I will exalt my throne above the stars of God: I will sit also upon the mount of the congregation, in the sides of the north: I will ascend above the heights of the clouds; I will be like the most High. Yet thou shalt be brought down to hell, to the sides of the pit. They that see thee shall narrowly look upon thee, and consider thee, saying, Is this the man that made the earth to tremble, that did shake kingdoms; That made the world as a wilderness, and destroyed the cities thereof; that opened not the house of his prisoners? All the kings of the nations, even all of them, lie in glory, every one in his own house. But thou art cast out of thy grave like an abominable branch, and as the raiment of those that are slain, thrust through with a sword, that go down to the stones of the pit; as a carcase trodden under feet.*

Spend your life serving Jesus. Why waste your life serving someone who hates you, deceives you, and will ultimately doom you?

## Points to Ponder and Discuss

1. Why is our personal testimony important in defeating our invisible enemy?

2. Explain what it means to live life with a "martyr's mentality."

3. Would you be willing to die for Jesus? Are you willing to live for Him?

# -10-
# Satan's Invisible Attacks (Part 1)

*By feeling Satan's fiery darts, we know assuredly that there is a Devil .* — George Whitefield

## Lesson Goals
1.  To understand the ways the Devil attacks the church
2.  To understand how to correctly respond to these attacks
3.  To be better equipped to help others who are experiencing satanic attacks

## Satan's Five Invisible Attacks Against the Church

***Revelation 12:17*** *And the dragon was wroth with the woman, and went to make war with the remnant of her seed, which keep the commandments of God, and have the testimony of Jesus Christ.*

Because Satan is invisible, his attacks against us are sometimes hard to identify. Satan may be the only person who doesn't want credit for the work he does! He wants to stir up problems in your life, then convince you that someone else is to blame. God's Word reveals to us the methods the Devil uses to attack the church, and many of these attacks are directed specifically at the young people of the church.

## 1.  Satan Wrestles Against the Brethren.
***Ephesians 6:10-13*** *Finally, my brethren, be strong in the Lord, and in the power of his might. Put on the whole armour of God, that ye may be able to stand against the wiles of the devil. For we wrestle not*

*against flesh and blood, but against principalities, against powers, against the rulers of the darkness of this world, against spiritual wickedness in high places. Wherefore take unto you the whole armour of God, that ye may be able to withstand in the evil day, and having done all, to stand.*

**Satan's Method:** Satan wants to get you into a wrestling match. He loves to instigate conflict and then convince you that your enemy is another person (flesh and blood). If he can keep you engaged in conflict with other people, then he can keep you distracted from serving the Lord.

Sometimes these "wrestling matches" are fought in our minds. If you think of a wrestling match, you think of an opponent who keeps you fully engaged, fully occupied, and whose efforts sap your strength. The enemy's goal is to "pin you onto the mat" so that you are neutralized. Satan will try to engage us in mental, emotional, or spiritual wrestling matches. He wants to occupy our minds with things that literally wear us out mentally, emotionally and spiritually. Envy, jealousy, self-doubt, anger, hatred, bitterness – all these things we "wrestle" with keep us so bound that we have little strength and energy to worship and serve the Lord. Satan introduces these mental sins into our thoughts, and if we do not respond properly, they can "pin us" for days and keep us ineffective for the Lord.

**Our Response:** The Scripture teaches us that we should avoid these wrestling matches by taking on the whole armor of God. Want to win a wrestling match with the Devil? Bring a sword!

***Ephesians 6:14-17*** *Stand therefore, having your loins girt about with truth, and having on the breastplate of righteousness; And your feet shod with the* *preparation of the gospel of peace; Above all, taking the shield of faith, wherewith ye shall be able to quench all the fiery darts of the wicked. And take the helmet of salvation, and the sword of the Spirit, which is the word of God:*

Nowhere in the Bible do we find that God intends for us to wrestle the Devil. When the Devil wants to wrestle, you pull out a sword! Satan cannot long stand up against the Word of God. Jesus taught us how to defeat the Devil during His forty days of temptation in the wilderness. Thrice the Son of God quoted the Scriptures, then He rebuked the Devil – "get behind me Satan."

Do you wrestle against envy? How about anger or bitterness or self-doubt? Memorize three verses that condemn these sinful mindsets (that the Devil tries to introduce into your thinking) and the minute you realize what he is doing, pull out the sword and stick him with it! Quote the Scriptures and rebuke him in Jesus' name.

***James 4:7*** *Submit yourselves therefore to God. Resist the devil, and he will flee from you.*

***1 Peter 5:8-9*** *Be sober, be vigilant; because your adversary the devil, as a roaring lion, walketh about, seeking whom he may devour: Whom resist stedfast in the faith, knowing that the same afflictions are accomplished in your brethren that are in the world.*

## 2. Satan Hinders Those Who Are Trying to Serve the Lord

***1 Thessalonians 2:17-18*** *But we, brethren, being taken from you for a short time in presence, not in heart, endeavoured the more abundantly to see your face with great desire. Wherefore we would have come unto you, even I Paul, once and again; but Satan hindered us.*

**Satan's Method:** Paul and his companions were trying to serve the Lord. They were first-century missionaries, evangelists, and church planters. Through inspiration, Paul mentions Satan from time to time would hinder their efforts. Paul wanted to come to Thessalonica to perfect that which was lacking in their faith, *"but Satan hindered us."*

The word *hindered* in this verse means "to cut into (figurative), to impede, to detain or to be tedious unto." It carries the idea of getting in front of someone and slowing them down or detaining them. Have you ever been driving somewhere, and you are in a hurry to get there? Inevitably, that is when you get behind someone that wants to drive 20 miles per hour UNDER the speed limit. And it seems this always happens on a winding stretch of road where it is impossible to pass them!

Satan sometimes uses circumstances beyond our control to slow our spiritual progress or even to stop us for a time. As we serve the Lord, the Devil will always try to put obstacles in our way to hinder our progress. Whether it be a Sunday School teacher trying to build his class, or a bus captain trying to reach an area for Christ, the Devil will always try to put up roadblocks to discourage and frustrate us.

**Our Response:** In order to overcome these attempts, we have to exercise patience. At times, there is nothing else we can do. The Christian's progress can be three steps forward and two steps backward. We must be patient, and we must not quit!

*Hebrews 12:1-2 Wherefore seeing we also are compassed about with so great a cloud of witnesses, let us lay aside every weight, and the sin which doth so easily beset us, **and let us run with patience the race that is set before us**, Looking unto Jesus the author and fin-*

isher of our faith; who for the joy that was set before him endured the cross, despising the shame, and is set down at the right hand of the throne of God.

The Christian life is not a sprint, it is a marathon. It seems odd to see the words *run* and *patience* in the same phrase. Long distance running requires the ability to pace oneself. It requires patience.

As you grow in grace, there will be setbacks along the way. There are times when circumstances make it such that you cannot progress at the rate you wish you could. Satan will do everything he can to hinder you so that you will get frustrated and discouraged. His goal is to get you to quit. Don't let him achieve that goal!!! Pray for strength and press forward! God will reward your faithfulness and give you the victory.

***2 Corinthians 4:8-10*** *We are troubled on every side, yet not distressed; we are perplexed, but not in despair; Persecuted, but not forsaken; cast down, but not destroyed; Always bearing about in the body the dying of the Lord Jesus, that the life also of Jesus might be made manifest in our body.*

## 3. Satan Sows Tares Among the Wheat

***Matthew 13:24-30*** *Another parable put he forth unto them, saying, The kingdom of heaven is likened unto a man which sowed good seed in his field: But while men slept, his enemy came and sowed tares among the wheat, and went his way. But when the blade was sprung up, and brought forth fruit, then appeared the tares also. So the servants of the householder came and said unto him, Sir, didst not thou sow good seed in thy field? from whence then hath it tares? He said unto them, An enemy hath done this. The servants said unto him, Wilt thou then that we go and gather them up? But he said, Nay; lest while ye gather up the tares, ye root* *up also the wheat with them. Let both grow together un-til the harvest: and in the time of harvest I will say to the reapers, Gather ye together first the tares, and bind them in bundles to burn them: but gather the wheat into my barn.*

*Matthew 13:36-43 Then Jesus sent the multitude away, and went into the house: and his disciples came unto him, saying, Declare unto us the parable of the tares of the field. He answered and said unto them, He that soweth the good seed is the Son of man; The field is the world; the good seed are the children of the king-dom; but the tares are the children of the wicked one; The enemy that sowed them is the devil; the harvest is the end of the world; and the reapers are the angels. As therefore the tares are gathered and burned in the fire; so shall it be in the end of this world...*

**Satan's Method:** Sowing tares among wheat is one of Satan's most diabolical schemes. He does it be-cause, sadly, it almost always works. In the parable of the tares, the enemy sneaks in at night and sows tares among the wheat. Tares are a darnel, or false grain. Tares look like wheat, but do not produce fruit. By the time you realize they are not really wheat, their roots have so intertwined with the roots of the wheat, that it is impossible to pull them up without damaging the grain-bearing plants.

The Devil will always plant his children amongst true Christians. They are not always easy to spot, be-cause some lost people can appear outwardly to be saved. Some lost people pick up the Christian lingo, dress, and behavior. They conform outwardly but have never been transformed inwardly.

**Our Response:** The only way to really spot a tare is to inspect his or her fruit!

***Matthew 7:15-20*** *Beware of false prophets, which come to you in sheep's clothing, but inwardly they are ravening wolves. Ye shall know them by their fruits. Do men gather grapes of thorns, or figs of thistles? Even so every good tree bringeth forth good fruit; but a corrupt tree bringeth forth evil fruit. A good tree cannot bring forth evil fruit, neither can a corrupt tree bring forth good fruit. Every tree that bringeth not forth good fruit is hewn down, and cast into the fire. Wherefore by their fruits ye shall know them.*

As a young person, you have to be wise enough to understand that there WILL ALWAYS BE PRETENDERS IN EVERY CHURCH. Watch for the young people who change who they are depending on who they are around. There is a difference between BEING a Christian and PLAYING a Christian. If someone puts on a show for adults, for the pastor, or for those in authority, then becomes someone evil and corrupt behind their backs, then mark them as a tare.

Do not create close friendships with pretenders. Don't be close enough to them to mix your roots with theirs. Seek out Christian friends who are genuine and sincere.

***Proverbs 27:17*** *Iron sharpeneth iron; so a man sharpeneth the countenance of his friend.*

***Psalm 119:63*** *I am a companion of all them that fear thee, and of them that keep thy precepts.*

***Proverbs 13:20*** *He that walketh with wise men shall be wise: but a companion of fools shall be destroyed.*

Remember, Satan is the master deceiver. We must be aware of how he works. Don't engage in a wrestling match with the Devil – instead, use your sword! Understand that he will try to hinder you as you serve the Lord, and sometimes you just have to exercise patience.  Also, be aware that not everyone who claims to be saved truly is.  Choose carefully your friends.

## Points to Ponder and Discuss

1.  What sin are you wrestling with?  Can you find three verses to memorize that will help you overcome?

2.  What is the difference between judging someone and inspecting their fruit?

3.  Think of a time when the Devil hindered you or your family by putting up a roadblock to try to prevent you from serving the Lord.

# -11-
# Satan's Invisible Attacks (Part 2)

*I know well that when Christ is nearest,
Satan also is busiest. — Robert Murray McCheyne*

## Lesson Goals
1. Review the three attacks in the previous lesson.
2. Learn to prevent Satan from stealing God's truths from our hearts.
3. Learn to recognize seducing spirits and doctrines of devils.

## Satan's Five Invisible Attacks Against the Church (continued)

### 4. Satan Seeks to Steal the Word of God from the Hearts of Young People
*Matthew 13:1-4* *...And he spake many things unto them in parables, saying, Behold, a sower went forth to sow; And when he sowed, some seeds fell by the way side, and the fowls came and devoured them up:*

*Matthew 13:18-19* *Hear ye therefore the parable of the sower. When any one heareth the word of the kingdom, and understandeth it not, then cometh the wicked one, and catcheth away that which was sown in his heart. This is he which received seed by the way side.*

**Satan's Method:** Satan hates the Word of God. He will do anything and everything he can to prevent the truths of the Bible from taking root in the heart of a young person.

*Satan battles us mentally as we try to read the Bible each day.* Have you ever experienced this? You begin to read your Bible, and after about two verses your mind begins to wander. You suddenly realize that you have "read" an entire chapter and have not comprehended a word of it! Satan caught away that which was meant for your heart.

*Satan battles us mentally as we try to listen to the Word of God taught and preached.* Again, the Devil will do anything to distract us from listening in church.

**Our Response:** We must learn to give our best attention to the Word of God, and seek not just to listen, but to understand what the Bible says, and what the preacher is saying about it. Before we read the Bible, or hear it preached, we should always ask the Holy Spirit to teach us something during our time with the Word.

*Our best focus should be given to our Bible reading.* Read your Bible with a pen and a 3x5 card in your hand. Look for what God will show you as you read. Underline key verses that speak to your heart. Jot down a verse or two to carry with you that day so that you can meditate upon them. If necessary, read the Bible out loud. This will help your mind not to wander.

*Our best focus should be given as we listen to the Bible taught or preached.* Sit as close to the front of the church as you can to minimize distractions. Again, have a pen and paper and jot down some key thoughts as you listen. Be tender to what God will teach you, and be ready to respond as the Holy Spirit so directs you.

## 5. Satan Introduces False Doctrine into the Minds of Young People

*1 Timothy 4:1-7    Now the Spirit speaketh expressly, that in the latter times some shall depart from the faith, giving heed to seducing spirits, and doctrines of devils; Speaking lies in hypocrisy; having their con-science seared with a hot iron; Forbidding to marry, and commanding to abstain from meats, which God hath created to be received with thanksgiving of them which believe and know the truth.... But refuse profane and old wives' fables, and exercise thyself rather unto godliness.*

**Satan's Method:** The Devil wants to cause young people to depart from the faith. Sadly, he has been effective at doing this. It is sad, because we have been warned WHAT he will try to do and HOW he will try to do it. The Devil attacks people using two danger-ous weapons: seducing spirits and doctrines of devils.

*Seducing spirits* are demonic spirits that wander the earth trying to impersonate the work of the Holy Spirit. They are imposters, sent to seduce Christians in-to believing false doctrine.

*Doctrines of devils* are teachings that are devilish in nature. It is teaching that is contrary to the Bible, or based on an improper interpretation of the Bible.

**Our Response:** Devilish doctrine empowered by seducing spirits is extremely dangerous! In order to re-spond correctly, we need to be able to recognize this di-abolical duo. The Bible goes on to describe them.

*A) "Speaking lies"* – God deals in truth, the Dev-il always deals in lies. Remember, honesty is telling the truth, the whole truth, and nothing but the truth. Many of the Devil's lies are disguised as partial truths or em-bellished truths. Make sure all instruction is based safe-ly and solidly on the truths of the Word of God.

*B) "In hypocrisy"* – One of the attributes of false teachers is that they are invariably hypocritical. Re-member, no one is perfect, but a man or woman whose life is in direct contradiction to the Scriptures has no business teaching anyone about what the Bible says.

*C) "Having their conscience seared with a hot iron..."* The conscience here is talking about our moral conscience. Devilish doctrine always seeks to break down Biblical moral boundaries by making us insensitive to worldliness and sin. Remember, true wisdom is first pure! Beware of any teaching that breaks down the boundaries of purity.

***James 3:17*** *But the wisdom that is from above is first pure, then peaceable, gentle, and easy to be intreated, full of mercy and good fruits, without partiality, and without hypocrisy.*

*D) "Forbidding to marry, and commanding to abstain from meats..."* Devilish doctrines always contain some extreme, unbiblical teachings. Forbidding marriage, or insisting people become vegetarians are examples of unscriptural boundaries. God encourages marriage, and has clearly sanctioned the eating of meat. Be careful of teachings that encourage behavior that God has condemned, or teachings that condemn behavior that God has encouraged.

*E) "But refuse profane and old wives' fables, and exercise thyself rather unto godliness."* Profane fables are based on heathen or pagan practices, and old wives' fables are based on myths or silly notions. We are commanded to refuse both. Instead, we are to exercise ourselves unto godliness.

## Points to Ponder and Discuss

1. Can you remember one truth from the last sermon you heard? If not, then what happened?

2. How can exercising oneself unto godliness insulate you from profane and old wives' fables?

# -12-
# Satan's Invisible Attacks (Part 3)

*To have grieved my God is the worst grief to me.*
*— Charles Spurgeon*

## Lesson Goals
1. Review the first five invisible attacks of Satan.
2. To warn young ladies of ways Satan gets to them
3. To evaluate our relationship with the Holy Spirit

Let's look at the last two ways Satan attacks young people.

## 6. Satan Tries to Misdirect Christian Young Ladies

*1 Timothy 5:9-15   Let not a widow be taken into the number under threescore years old, having been the wife of one man,... But the younger widows refuse: for when they have begun to wax wanton against Christ, they will marry; Having damnation, because they have cast off their first faith. And withal they learn to be idle, wandering about from house to house; and not only idle, but tattlers also and busybodies, speaking things which they ought not. I will therefore that the younger women marry, bear children, guide the house, give none occasion to the adversary to speak reproachfully. For some are already turned aside after Satan.*

**Satan's Method:** Satan wants to corrupt young ladies – to get them to *"turn aside after Satan."* He does this by misdirecting them from their God-given purpose to his perverted purposes.

*1. Satan wants to misdirect young ladies from*

*their first faith.* To "cast off" means to set aside, disesteem, or neutralize. Satan wants to destroy the sweetness and excitement that every young person experiences when they first get saved.

*2. Satan wants to misdirect young ladies from good works to idleness.* A virtuous young lady stays busy on purpose. She finds things to do that will be a blessing to her family, her parents and her church. Satan wants to replace these good works with time spent in selfishness and sin.

*3. Satan wants to misdirect young ladies from purpose to wandering.* A noble life is lived on purpose, for a cause bigger than oneself. If you have no cause, then you have no direction.

*4. Satan wants to misdirect young ladies from quietness to tattling.* Tattling is prating. Prating is idle conversation and empty words. Satan wants you to spend your life engaged in conversations that are empty of value and sprinkled with sin.

**1 Peter 3:4** *...the ornament of a meek and quiet spirit, which is in the sight of God of great price.*

**Proverbs 10:8** *The wise in heart will receive commandments: but a prating fool shall fall.*

*5. Satan wants to misdirect young ladies from serving to snooping.* A tattler always, eventually, becomes a busybody. Satan wants to get you to spend your time becoming a gossiping busybody. This type of a young lady is a poor testimony for the Lord.

**Our Response:** A young lady must guard against sins that cause her to turn aside after Satan.

*1. Guard carefully the sweetness of your faith.* Always maintain a thankful spirit toward God for the wonderful salvation bought for us by the sacrifice of His Son, Jesus Christ.

*2. Stay busy serving the Lord!* Do not let idleness creep into your life.

    *3. Live on purpose for a purpose!* Lose yourself in winning others to Christ and being a blessing to those who are saved.

    *4. Study to be quiet.* Don't get caught up in all the idle gossip whirling around.

    *5. Guard against becoming a busybody.* Learn to mind your own business. Don't involve yourself in the affairs of others.

## 7. Satan Tries to Destroy a Christian's Relationship with the Holy Spirit.

    ***Acts 5:9*** *...Peter said unto her, How is it that ye have agreed together to tempt the Spirit of the Lord? behold, the feet of them which have buried thy husband are at the door, and shall carry thee out.*

    **Satan's Method:** Satan wants to damage the relationship you have with the Holy Spirit. Remember, if you are saved, the Holy Spirit indwells you. Satan cannot change this, but he will try to get you to live a life that will grieve, quench, and eventually tempt the Holy Spirit of God.

    *1. Satan wants you to grieve the Holy Spirit.* Anytime Satan can get you to live in disobedience to the Scriptures, it affects the relationship you have to the Spirit of God. The Holy Spirit is grieved when we sin, and He convicts us of that sin. When we willfully sin, and refuse His reproof, we grieve His heart.

    ***Ephesians 4:30*** *And grieve not the holy Spirit of God, whereby ye are sealed unto the day of redemption.*

    *2. Satan wants you to quench the Holy Spirit.* Christians who constantly ignore the Spirit of God can get to the point where they quench His voice in their lives. Grieving leads to quenching. To hear the convicting voice of the Holy Spirit and then to ignore it is a dangerous thing!  Soon, His voice will grow quieter and, if we are not careful, can be altogether quenched.

*1 Thessalonians 5:19   Quench not the Spirit.*

3.  *Satan wants you to tempt the Holy Spirit.*  If we grieve the Spirit, then quench the Spirit, the next step is that we begin to tempt the Spirit.  Ananias and Sapphira had their lives cut short because they allowed Satan to fill their hearts to lie to the Holy Spirit.  If you are not careful, your entire life can soon become a lie!  Be careful!  God is no respecter of persons.  If you are truly a child of God, you place yourself in grave danger when you live a life that brings open shame to Christ.

**Our Response:**  Your relationship with the Holy Spirit ought to be treated very sacredly.  God placed His Spirit inside of you to seal you till the day of redemption.  The Holy Spirit guides us to divine appointments so that we can witness to people whose hearts are prepared to receive the Gospel.  He is also there to comfort you, to tutor you as you study the Scriptures, and to be your prayer partner.  But He is also there to convict you and to rebuke you when you sin.  Do not harden your heart to His reproofs!  Be tender and responsive to His leading in your life.

When we properly respond to the conviction of the Holy Spirit, we avoid grieving Him.  This guards us against getting on the road that leads to quenching and tempting the Holy Spirit.

## Points to Ponder and Discuss

1.  How has the Devil used today's technology to increase the temptation to become a tattler and busy body?

2.  In what ways does the Devil try to keep you from having a close relationship with the Holy Spirit?

# -13-
# Satan's Invisible Army (Part 1)

*It was pride that changed angels into devils.*
*— Augustine*

## Lesson Goals
1. To understand the origin of demons/devils
2  To understand why they are so successful at what they do
3. To understand the character traits of a demonic stronghold

*Revelation 12:3-4  And there appeared another wonder in heaven; and behold a great red dragon, having seven heads and ten horns, and seven crowns upon his heads.  And his tail drew the third part of the stars of heaven, and did cast them to the earth: and the dragon stood before the woman which was ready to be delivered, for to devour her child as soon as it was born.*

When Satan fell from Heaven, he deceived one third of God's angels into following him into rebellion. These fallen angels, or devils, have now become the servants of Satan.  They assist him in trying to destroy the souls of the lost, and fight against the church of Jesus Christ.

## 1. Devils are Many
*Hebrews 12:22  But ye are come unto mount Sion, and unto the city of the living God, the heavenly Jerusalem, and to an innumerable company of angels,*

The Bible describes the angels of Heaven as

"innumerable." Satan carried away one third of this innumerable host! That means there are many devils under his control.

## Where Are These Devils Today?

*1. Many devils are active here on Earth doing the bidding of their evil master.*

*1 Timothy 4:1 Now the Spirit speaketh expressly, that in the latter times some shall depart from the faith, giving heed to seducing spirits, and doctrines of devils.*

*2. Some devils are chained, awaiting judgment.*

*Jude 1:6 And the angels which kept not their first estate, but left their own habitation, he hath reserved in everlasting chains under darkness unto the judgment of the great day.*

*2 Peter 2:4 For if God spared not the angels that sinned, but cast them down to hell, and delivered them into chains of darkness, to be reserved unto judgment;*

*3. Some devils, who are now chained, will be released during the tribulation period.*

*Revelation 9:1-11 And the fifth angel sounded, and I saw a star fall from heaven unto the earth: and to him was given the key of the bottomless pit. And he opened the bottomless pit; and there arose a smoke out of the pit, as the smoke of a great furnace; and the sun and the air were darkened by reason of the smoke of the pit. And there came out of the smoke locusts upon the earth: and unto them was given power, as the scorpions of the earth have power... And they had tails like unto scorpions, and there were stings in their tails: and their power was to hurt men five months. And they had a king over them, which is the angel of the bottomless pit, whose name in the Hebrew tongue is Abaddon, but in the Greek tongue hath his name Apollyon.*

Despite the many devils chained and awaiting judgment, there are still untold thousands of fallen angels who roam the earth, fighting the Lord's church.

## 2. Devils are Loyal

*Mark 3:22-26 And the scribes which came down from Jerusalem said, He hath Beelzebub, and by the prince of the devils casteth he out devils. And he called them unto him, and said unto them in parables, How can Satan cast out Satan? And if a kingdom be divided against itself, that kingdom cannot stand. And if a house be divided against itself, that house cannot stand. And if Satan rise up against himself, and be divided, he cannot stand, but hath an end.*

Satan's house is not divided. The devils are loyal to Satan, and work together to do his bidding. How sad that devils can be loyal and work together, while many church congregations are disloyal to their pastor and uncooperative in their efforts to evangelize.

## 3. Devils are Organized

*Ephesians 6:12 For we wrestle not against flesh and blood, but against principalities, against powers, against the rulers of the darkness of this world, against spiritual wickedness in high places.*

Satan will never be accused of being disorganized. Not only are his followers loyal, they are also very well organized.

*1. Principalities:* Satan has ruling magistrates. This means that some devils oversee large divisions of followers. The devils are organized in military fashion.

*2. Powers:* Some devils have delegated influence and mastery. These devils are like Satan's elite forces. Again, this is likened to our military's special forces units.

**3. *Rulers of the darkness of this world:*** Satan has geographically-placed satanic rulers. Remember, unlike God, the Devil is not omnipresent. He cannot be in more than one place at once. So, having strategically placed generals is a must.

**4. *Spiritual wickedness in high places:*** These are supernaturally depraved plotters. They are in charge of coordinating attacks upon Godly strongholds.

Organization is one of the most important aspects of warfare. Satan commands a very efficient and very well-organized army of devils.

## 4. Devils Create Strong Holds

***Revelation 2:12-13*** *And to the angel of the church in Pergamos write; These things saith he which hath the sharp sword with two edges; I know thy works and where thou dwellest, even where Satan's seat is: and thou holdest fast my name, and hast not denied my faith, even in those days wherein Antipas was my faithful martyr, who was slain among you, where Satan dwelleth.*

Pergamos means "fortified." This city was at one time a satanic stronghold. A satanic stronghold is a geographic location where there is a concentration of demonic activity. This can be a city, a region, or even a country. Pergamos was not only a stronghold, but at this time was the location of Satan's throne. Remember, Satan is not omnipresent. He can only be in one place at one time. This was his demonic headquarters on Earth, and yet there was a church in this city winning people to Christ!

No one knows where Satan's seat is today. Is it New York City, Las Vegas, or Washington? Does Satan reside in Rome, Moscow, Beijing, or Jerusalem? We know he is somewhere! And we also know that there are, without doubt, satanic strongholds.

What are the characteristics of a stronghold?

1. *Concentration of demonic activity.*
2. *Concentration of occult activity.*
3. *Concentration of people enslaved to sin.*
4. *Concentration of false religions.*
5. *Concentration of persecution of Christians.*

These areas need a gospel light! Be sure to pray for your missionaries. Many of them are laboring in areas that are demonic strongholds. Churches can and should be started right in the Devil's backyard! But remember, Satan will not easily surrender places that have taken him hundreds of years to secure.

## 5. Some Devils Can Work Miracles

*Exodus 7:10-13    And Moses and Aaron went in unto Pharaoh, and they did so as the LORD had commanded: and Aaron cast down his rod before Pharaoh, and before his servants, and it became a serpent. Then Pharaoh also called the wise men and the sorcerers: now the magicians of Egypt, they also did in like manner with their enchantments. For they cast down every man his rod, and they became serpents: but Aaron's rod swallowed up their rods. And he hardened Pharaoh's heart, that he hearkened not unto them; as the LORD had said.*

*Exodus 7:20-22    And Moses and Aaron did so, as the LORD commanded; and he lifted up the rod, and smote the waters that were in the river, in the sight of Pharaoh, and in the sight of his servants; and all the waters that were in the river were turned to blood. And the fish that was in the river died; and the river stank, and the Egyptians could not drink of the water of the river; and there was blood throughout all the land of Egypt. And the magicians of Egypt did so with their en-*

*chantments: and Pharaoh's heart was hardened, neither did he hearken unto them; as the LORD had said.*

*Exodus 8:16-19   And the LORD said unto Moses, Say unto Aaron, Stretch out thy rod, and smite the dust of the land, that it may become lice throughout all the land of Egypt. And they did so; for Aaron stretched out his hand with his rod, and smote the dust of the earth, and it became lice in man, and in beast; all the dust of the land became lice throughout all the land of Egypt. And the magicians did so with their enchantments to bring forth lice, but they could not: so there were lice upon man, and upon beast. Then the magicians said unto Pharaoh, This is the finger of God: and Pharaoh's heart was hardened, and he hearkened not unto them; as the LORD had said.*

God gave Moses and Aaron the ability to perform miracles. We read that Pharaoh then called his "magicians" to duplicate these miracles. And they did! However, as we compare the two, we see some glaring differences between God's miracles and the devils' miracles.

***1. Devilish miracles are inferior to God's miracles.*** Both Aaron and the magicians turned rods into serpents, but Aaron's serpent "swallowed up" their serpents.

***2. Devilish miracles are harmful to those who perform them.*** By mimicking the miracle of turning water into blood, they added to their own misery. *"... and the fish that was in the river died; and the river stank, and the Egyptians could not drink of the waters of the river..."*

***3. Devilish miracles are limited; God's miracles have no limits.*** At some point, the magicians could not match the miracles of God. They had to admit God's superiority to Pharaoh, *"This is the finger of God!"* Sadly though, some people are still deceived by demonic miracles! The Bible cautions us to try the spirits to see if they are from Satan or from God.

*1 John 4:1    Beloved, believe not every spirit, but try the spirits whether they are of God: because many false prophets are gone out into the world.*

Many false, contemporary churches claim that you can really "feel the spirit" in their church. What we should remember is that God's true Spirit has a first name – He is called the HOLY Spirit. Not all spiritual activity is from God. The Holy Spirit produces a holy atmosphere. And He promotes personal holiness in our lives.

It should not surprise us that, during the tribulation period, there will be many miracles produced by false prophets.

*Revelation 16:13-14    And I saw three unclean spirits like frogs come out of the mouth of the dragon, and out of the mouth of the beast, and out of the mouth of the false prophet. For they are the spirits of devils, working miracles, which go forth unto the kings of the earth and of the whole world, to gather them to the battle of that great day of God Almighty.*

Satan's army of devils are many, they are loyal, and they are organized. They work in military fashion to create strong-holds. They also have the ability to mimic the miracles of God in order to deceive people into believing they are from above.

## Points to Ponder and Discuss

1. What character traits make devils so successful?

2. Discuss the character traits of a satanic stronghold.

3. How can satanic strongholds be reached with the Gospel of Jesus Christ? (Hint: in a recent study, what three things overcame the wicked one?)

# -14-
# Satan's Invisible Army (Part 2)

*One touch of Christ is worth a lifetime of struggling.*
*— A. B. Simpson*

**Lesson Goals**
1. Review last week's lesson.
2. To learn the character traits associated with demonic possession or oppression
3. To receive assurance of God's power over devils

Let's study more attributes of Satan's invisible army of demons.

## 6. Devils Seek to Oppress and Possess the Lost

*Acts 10:38 How God anointed Jesus of Nazareth with the Holy Ghost and with power: who went about doing good, and healing all that were oppressed of the devil; for God was with him.*

A large part of Christ's earthly ministry was healing people who were either possessed or oppressed by devils. Let's examine the encounter between Christ and the maniac of Gadara, and list the symptoms of those who are demon possessed.

*Luke 8:26-35 And they arrived at the country of the Gadarenes, which is over against Galilee. And when he went forth to land, there met him out of the city a certain man, which had devils long time, and ware no clothes, neither abode in any house, but in the tombs. When he saw Jesus, he cried out, and fell down before him, and with a loud voice said, What have I to do with thee, Jesus, thou Son of God most high? I beseech thee, torment me not. (For he had commanded the unclean spirit to come out of the man. For oftentimes it had caught him: and he was kept bound with chains and in fetters; and he brake the bands, and was driven of the devil into the wilderness.) And Jesus asked him, saying, What is thy name? And he said, Legion: because many devils were entered into him... Then they went out to see what was done; and came to Jesus, and found the man, out of whom the devils were departed, sitting at the feet of Jesus, clothed, and in his right mind: and they were afraid.*

**1. Demonic activity produces nakedness.** (Verse 27) This man *"ware no clothes."* The more Satan has laid claim to the culture, the more we have accepted and excused immodesty.

**2. Demonic activity produces homelessness.** (Verse 27) The Bible says that this man *"neither abode in any house."* Those who work with homeless people will attest to the fact that a large number turn down housing opportunities! Much of the mental illness associated with the homeless is really demonic oppression.

**3. Demonic activity creates an infatuation with death.** (Verse 27) This man chose to dwell *"in the tombs."* Our culture's infatuation with death is well documented. Gothic styles, skulls, ghost hunting, and, sadly, suicide are becoming normal today. Music and movies strongly reflect the demonic activity of our times.

**4. Demonic activity results in uncontrolled fits of anger.** (Verse 29) It is said of this man that often these devils *"caught him."* Often he became destructive and violent. More and more young people are being sent to "anger management classes" when the answer to their problems would be found if their parents sent them instead to Sunday School!

**5. Demonic activity results in imprisonment.**

(Verse 29) The community finally had to chain him! Our prisons are filled with people who are so controlled by devils that there becomes nothing left to do but put them in a cage. All kinds of attempts are made to rehabilitate them, when they really just need Jesus!

**6. Demonic activity sometimes exhibits itself in superhuman strength.** (Verse 29) This poor possessed man broke the chains and fetters with which they tried to bind him! Check out the music that many of our professional athletes are listening to just before taking to the field of competition. Many are attempting to channel an "inner strength and power" that they may not even realize is dangerously demonic.

**7. Demonic activity results in bizarre, insane behavior.** (Verse 29) This man had to be driven into the wilderness. With the increase of demonic activity in these last days, more and more people are suffering from mental issues. They are given drugs that, in many cases, create the potential for even more violent or self-destructive behavior! There is help!!! But it is not found in a bottle, it is found in the Bible! Jesus is the answer.

**8. Demonic activity results in exceedingly fierce and violent tendencies.** (Mt 8:28) Matthew's account tells us the man was *"exceeding fierce, so that no man might pass by that way."* He was dangerous to innocent people. He would aggressively attack those who passed by. More and more newspaper headlines are filled with people just "going off" and committing acts of random violence. It's impossible to deny the Devil's part in this.

**9. Demonic activity sometimes results in self-mutilation and other forms of self-destructive behavior.** (Mark 5:5) Mark's account tells us this man engaged in *"crying and cutting himself with stones."* Self-mutilation has become a national epidemic with young people. Self-destructive behavior, including drug and alcohol abuse, eating disorders, and "cutting," is very common in our times. This, again, is evidence of the growing number of people who are falling under satanic oppression.

**10. Demonic activity results in suicidal thoughts and attempts.** Sadly, some of these result in death. Jesus had a father bring a demon-possessed child to Him to see if Jesus could help the boy. One of the things the father told Jesus was that the Devil drove the boy to suicide attempts.

**Mark 9:22** *And ofttimes it hath cast him into the fire, and into the waters, to destroy him: but if thou canst do any thing, have compassion on us, and help us.*

Again, the number of suicides and suicide attempts continues to rise drastically as Satan is preparing the world for the tribulation period.

Is there an answer for devilish oppression? Notice the difference when the man came to Jesus!

**Luke 8:35** *Then they went out to see what was done; and came to Jesus, and found the man, out of whom the devils were departed, sitting at the feet of Jesus, clothed, and in his right mind: and they were afraid.*

## 7. Devils Fight Against the Work of God

**1 Timothy 4:1** *Now the Spirit speaketh expressly, that in the latter times some shall depart from the faith, giving heed to seducing spirits, and doctrines of devils;*

The devils also come to the house of the Lord! They do not just try to destroy the lost, they try to disrupt the saved. One man said this: ***The number on your church's attendance board only reveals the number of those in attendance from the visible creation. If most of us could see all who were in attendance each Sunday – both good and evil – from the invisible creation, it would drive the church to its knees in prayer!***

The Devil sends his army to fight against every

Bible-preaching, soul-winning church. We should not be surprised when we are attacked; we should prepare for it and expect it!

## 8. Devils Believe in God

Devils are smarter than atheists! They believe in God, and have the sense to "*tremble*" at the mere mention of the Almighty.

*James 2:19* *Thou believest that there is one God; thou doest well: the devils also believe, and tremble.*

## 9. Devils Know Who Christ Is and Must Obey His Direct Commands

In the Gospels, when we read of the encounters between Jesus and devils, it is interesting to see their reaction and listen to what they say to the Son of God.

*Luke 4:31-35* *And came down to Capernaum, a city of Galilee, and taught them on the sabbath days. And they were astonished at his doctrine: for his word was with power. And in the synagogue there was a man, which had a spirit of an unclean devil, and cried out with a loud voice, Saying, Let us alone; what have we to do with thee, thou Jesus of Nazareth? art thou come to destroy us? I know thee who thou art; the Holy One of God. And Jesus rebuked him, saying, Hold thy peace, and come out of him. And when the devil had thrown him in the midst, he came out of him, and hurt him not.*

*Matthew 8:28-33* *So the devils besought him, saying, If thou cast us out, suffer us to go away into the herd of swine. And he said unto them, Go. And when they were come out, they went into the herd of swine: and, behold, the whole herd of swine ran violently down a steep place into the sea, and perished in the waters. And they that kept them fled, and went their ways into the city, and told every thing, and what was befallen to the possessed of the devils.*

Again, devils are smarter than most people. Some men are so foolish as to deny that Jesus is the *"Holy One of God."* Other men refuse to obey His Word. Demons know better than that!

These devils are powerless in the presence of our Lord! That should give us great comfort.

***1 John 4:4*** *Ye are of God, little children, and have overcome them: because greater is he that is in you, than he that is in the world.*

## 10. Devils Are Doomed

***Matthew 25:41*** *Then shall he say also unto them on the left hand, Depart from me, ye cursed, into everlasting fire, prepared for the devil and his angels:*

The Lake of Fire will be the final destination for Satan and his invisible army. Never forget, in the end, Jesus will be victorious! If you are saved and living for Jesus, then you are on the winning side.

It is important that we understand the power of this invisible army. Never underestimate their determination to destroy your life. Live in the Bible, live on your knees, and remember that you serve a Savior that is greater than them all.

## Points to Ponder and Discuss

1. What are the evidences of demonic activity in the lives of young people today?

2. How can Christians limit the activity of devils in disrupting the services in their local church?

3. In light of what we have learned about Satan's invisible army, why is it so important to stay close to God?

# -15-
# The Heavenly Cloud of Witnesses

*I am still in the land of the dying; I shall be in the land of the living soon. —John Newton's last words*

**Lesson Goals**
1. To Scripturally define the great "cloud of witnesses"
2. To be reminded of God's eyes upon us
3. To learn how to successfully run our race

*Hebrews 12:1-3    Wherefore seeing we also are compassed about with so great a cloud of witnesses, let us lay aside every weight, and the sin which doth so easily beset us, and let us run with patience the race that is set before us,  Looking unto Jesus the author and finisher of our faith; who for the joy that was set before him endured the cross, despising the shame, and is set down at the right hand of the throne of God.  For consider him that endured such contradiction of sinners against himself, lest ye be wearied and faint in your minds.*

One of the great motivational truths of the Bible is the fact that we are being observed by a heavenly host!  Heaven's occupants are very much interested in the race we are running.

## 1.  God is watching all we do.
*2 Chronicles 16:9    For the eyes of the LORD run to and fro throughout the whole earth, to shew himself strong in the behalf of them whose heart is perfect toward him...*
*Proverbs 5:21    For the ways of man are before the eyes of the LORD, and he pondereth all his goings.*

91

***Proverbs 15:3*** *The eyes of the LORD are in every place, beholding the evil and the good.*

There is no greater transforming truth for the Christian! God sees the good that we do. Men might not notice, but God sees all. God also sees the evil we do. There is no place to hide from Him. God is a just God who rewards good and punishes evil. Every day, we would be wise to walk in the knowledge of this great truth.

## 2. The angels are watching as well.

***1 Corinthians 4:9*** *For I think that God hath set forth us the apostles last, as it were appointed to death: for we are made a spectacle unto the world, and to angels, and to men.*

This fact should motivate us as Christians! Angels are a part of that great "cloud of witnesses" who are rooting for us to live for God. They especially enjoy and encourage our soul winning efforts. Angels respond with great joy to the salvation of a soul.

***Luke 15:10*** *Likewise, I say unto you, there is joy in the presence of the angels of God over one sinner that repenteth.*

## 3. Heaven's saints are rooting us on!

***Hebrews 12:1-3*** *Wherefore seeing we also are compassed about with so great a cloud of witnesses, let us lay aside every weight, and the sin which doth so easily beset us, and let us run with patience the race that is set before us, Looking unto Jesus the author and finisher of our faith; who for the joy that was set before him endured the cross, despising the shame, and is set down at the right hand of the throne of God. For consider him that endured such contradiction of sinners against himself, lest ye be wearied and faint in your minds.*

The "cloud of witnesses" are in part the men and

women of the previous chapter of Hebrews. The eleventh chapter of Hebrews, the great "faith chapter," contains a "Who's Who of Bible Heroes." Abel, Enoch, Noah, Abraham and Sarah, Isaac, Jacob, and Joseph are all now a part of the heavenly audience. Moses, Joshua, Rahab, Gideon and Samuel have run their race. All of these great Christians, and more, root us on, encouraging us to live for God. They now behold the face of our Savior and they know that it is worth it to serve God!

In addition to these who are listed, all of the faithful men and women of all the ages watch in hopes that we will not waste our time here. They know that life truly is a vapor that appears but for a short time then is gone. The song writer wrote, "Only one life so soon it will pass, only what's done for Christ will last!"

This great cloud of witnesses should encourage us to make several decisions about our lives.

### 1. Lay Aside Every Weight

**Hebrews 12:1** *Wherefore seeing we also are compassed about with so great a cloud of witnesses, let us lay aside every weight, and the sin which doth so easily beset us, and let us run with patience the race that is set before us,*

In order to properly and successfully run the race that is set before us, we have to be willing to lay aside every weight. A weight is any burden or any hindrance that might jeopardize our ability to finish the race. A weight is not the same as a sin. Some things are not sinful, but they do hinder us from having the time and energy to serve the Lord.

### 2. Lay Aside Your Besetting Sin

We are instructed to *"lay aside....the sin which doth so easily beset us."* Each Christian needs to identify what this sin is in his life and seek victory over it.

Different people are susceptible to different sins. Memorize the Scriptures you will need to battle your besetting sin, then make no provision for that sin in your life.

### 3. Run with Patience

The Christian life is not a sprint, it is a marathon. While running our race, we will need patience – patience with others and patience with ourselves. Some days we will struggle. At times we will fall. Every day must be viewed as a new chance, a new beginning. Every day is another leg of the race, and we should seek from God each morning the strength and grace to successfully run our race.

### 4. Keep Your Eyes on Jesus

**Hebrews 12:2-3**   *Looking unto Jesus the author and finisher of our faith; who for the joy that was set before him endured the cross, despising the shame, and is set down at the right hand of the throne of God. For consider him that endured such contradiction of sinners against himself, lest ye be wearied and faint in your minds.*

Jesus is our greatest inspiration! He did not quit! Jesus was a finisher. If we keep our eyes on Him, we will make it to the finish line.

A faithful, aged evangelist was asked the secret behind his longevity in the ministry and his faithfulness to God. His answer was a simple one, "Every morning I get up, look around till I see Jesus and head in that direction!"

## Points to Ponder and Discuss

1. What can we do daily to better remind ourselves of the truth of God's ever watchfulness?

2. What is the difference between a sin and a weight?

# *-16-*
# Heaven (Part 1)

*We'll say good night here, and*
*good morning up there.* —John R. Rice

## Lesson Goals
1. To learn of all the wonderful things awaiting us in Heaven
2. To give us comfort concerning those who are already there
3. To make us long for Heaven

The Bible gives us glimpses of Heaven. There is no way we can imagine all of its wonders! Let's take a look at what will be in Heaven, and what won't be in Heaven.

## What Will Be In Heaven?

### 1. The Throne of God

*Acts 7:55-56 But he, being full of the Holy Ghost, looked up stedfastly into heaven, and saw the glory of God, and Jesus standing on the right hand of God, And said, Behold, I see the heavens opened, and the Son of man standing on the right hand of God.*

God reigns supreme in Heaven! He sits upon His throne, and His will is honored and obeyed. In Heaven, Jehovah God receives the worship He deserves. The throne of God is described in great detail in the fourth chapter of Revelation.

*Revelation 4:1-11 After this I looked, and, behold, a door was opened in heaven: and the first voice* which I heard was as it were of a trumpet talking with me; which said, Come up hither, and I will shew thee things which must be hereafter. And immediately I was in the spirit: and, behold, a throne was set in heaven, and one sat on the throne. And he that sat was to look upon like a jasper and a sardine stone: and there was a rainbow round about the throne, in sight like unto an emerald. And round about the throne were four and twenty seats: and upon the seats I saw four and twenty elders sitting, clothed in white raiment; and they had on their heads crowns of gold. And out of the throne proceeded lightnings and thunderings and voices: and there were seven lamps of fire burning before the throne, which are the seven Spirits of God. And before the throne there was a sea of glass like unto crystal: and in the midst of the throne, and round about the throne, were four beasts full of eyes before and behind....

## 2. The Son of God

*Revelation 5:6-9* And I beheld, and, lo, in the midst of the throne and of the four beasts, and in the midst of the elders, stood a Lamb as it had been slain, having seven horns and seven eyes, which are the seven Spirits of God sent forth into all the earth. And he came and took the book out of the right hand of him that sat upon the throne. And when he had taken the book, the four beasts and four and twenty elders fell down before the Lamb, having every one of them harps, and golden vials full of odours, which are the prayers of saints. And they sung a new song, saying, Thou art worthy to take the book, and to open the seals thereof: for thou wast slain, and hast redeemed us to God by thy blood out of every kindred, and tongue, and people, and nation;

Jesus, the Lamb of God, awaits us in Heaven. Imagine getting to see the One who sacrificed Himself to open Heaven for us. One man said, "The only thing in Heaven made by man will be the nail scars in our Savior's hands." The song writer wrote, "Jesus will be what makes it Heaven for me!"

## 3. The Angels of God

*2 Kings 6:15-17* *And when the servant of the man of God was risen early, and gone forth, behold, an host compassed the city both with horses and chariots. And his servant said unto him, Alas, my master! how shall we do? And he answered, Fear not: for they that be with us are more than they that be with them. And Elisha prayed, and said, LORD, I pray thee, open his eyes, that he may see. And the LORD opened the eyes of the young man; and he saw: and, behold, the mountain was full of horses and chariots of fire round about Elisha.*

Elisha's servant was allowed a sneak preview of the host of Heaven. We can only imagine what it will be like to get to see the mighty host of angels who serve the Lord. Imagine getting to meet your guardian angel! We will get to join these angels in worshipping our Lord.

## 4. The Saints of All the Ages

*Matthew 8:11* *And I say unto you, That many shall come from the east and west, and shall sit down with Abraham, and Isaac, and Jacob, in the kingdom of heaven.*

*Matthew 17:1-3* *And after six days Jesus taketh Peter, James, and John his brother, and bringeth them up into an high mountain apart, And was transfigured before them: and his face did shine as the sun, and his raiment was white as the light. And, behold, there appeared unto them Moses and Elias talking with him.*

Heaven will be the great gathering place of the saints of all the ages. We will get to sit down with our

Bible heroes and hear from them firsthand the stories which we know so well. Christian men and women of every generation will be there. Martyrs and missionaries, prophets and preachers, evangelists and every-day men will gather to share the stories of the grace and mercy of God in their lives. And there will be time to spend with each and every one!

## 5. Pearly Gates, Golden Streets, and Mansions

*John 14:1-3   Let not your heart be troubled: ye believe in God, believe also in me. In my Father's house are many mansions: if it were not so, I would have told you. I go to prepare a place for you. And if I go and prepare a place for you, I will come again, and receive you unto myself; that where I am, there ye may be also.*

*Revelation 21:21   And the twelve gates were twelve pearls; every several gate was of one pearl: and the street of the city was pure gold, as it were transparent glass.*

Jesus has gone to prepare a place for us, and what a place! A mansion awaits us in Heaven. Can you imagine walking into that celestial city? Every one of us who are saved will one day walk through those gates of pearl, down streets that are paved with gold so pure that it will be like walking on glass. And lining these streets, mansions that will make the richest neighborhoods in America look like the ghetto!

## 6. The Holy Book, the Record Books, and the Book of Life!

*Psalm 119:89   For ever, O LORD, thy word is settled in heaven.*

*Mark 13:31   Heaven and earth shall pass away: but my words shall not pass away.*

The Bible will be in Heaven. God's precious Word is eternal. Satan has spent his life trying to destroy it here on Earth, but in the end it will be God's Word that destroys him!

*Philippians 4:3   And I entreat thee also, true yokefellow, help those women which laboured with me in the gospel, with Clement also, and with other my fellow labourers, whose names are in the book of life.*

*Revelation 20:12-15   And I saw the dead, small and great, stand before God; and the books were opened: and another book was opened, which is the book of life: and the dead were judged out of those things which were written in the books, according to their works.   And the sea gave up the dead which were in it; and death and hell delivered up the dead which were in them: and they were judged every man according to their works.   And death and hell were cast into the lake of fire. This is the second death.   And whosoever was not found written in the book of life was cast into the lake of fire.*

Accurate records are kept in Heaven.  A book of each of our lives records the deeds done while we lived out our time on Earth.  For the saved, all sin is blotted out by the blood of Christ!  Our sacrifice, service, stewardship and soul winning efforts are recorded so that proper rewards can be granted.  For the lost man, all of his sins await him, still recorded in the book of his life. Those sins he must face at the judgment seat.   Those sins he must pay for in the Lake of Fire forever.

The Book of Life accurately records the names of those who have received Jesus as their Savior.  Is your name written in the Book of Life?

## 7.  The River of Life and the Tree of Life

*Revelation 22:1-2   And he shewed me a pure river of water of life, clear as crystal, proceeding out of the throne of God and of the Lamb.   In the midst of the street of it, and on either side of the river, was there the tree of life, which bare twelve manner of fruits, and yielded her fruit every month: and the leaves of the tree were for the healing of the nations.*

Flowing from the throne of God is the river of water of life. There we can drink freely forever. And the tree of life grows beside the river of life. Every month, it yields a different manner of fruit. And forever, we are granted the privilege of eating from the tree of life. What a gathering place! Both of these are before the throne of God. Fellowship and food, water and worship, and all God's people before His throne enjoying eternity together!

## Points to Ponder and Discuss

1. What are you most looking forward to seeing in Heaven?

2. Whom are you most looking forward to seeing in Heaven?

3. Are you sure you are going to Heaven?

# -17-
# Heaven (Part 2)

*The Word of God tells us of the day when tears shall be gone forever. — Lee Roberson*

**Lesson Goals**
1. To study what will NOT be in Heaven
2. To make Heaven sweeter in our minds and hearts
3. To make us long for Heaven

Last week we studied what WILL be in Heaven, now let's look at what will NOT be in Heaven.

## What Will NOT Be In Heaven!

**1. No Death!**
**2. No Sorrow!**
**3. No Crying!**
**4. No Pain!**

*Revelation 21:4 And God shall wipe away all tears from their eyes; and there shall be no more death, neither sorrow, nor crying, neither shall there be any more pain: for the former things are passed away.*

No funeral homes, no goodbyes, no weeping, no despair, no hurting, no pain, no hospitals – all of these former things are passed away.

## 5. No Temple!

*Revelation 21:22 And I saw no temple therein: for the Lord God Almighty and the Lamb are the temple of it.*

There will be no need of an earthly, man-made structure where we gather for worship. Instead, all worship will take place before the throne of God.

## 6. No Sun, No Moon, No Electricity Needed!

*Revelation 21:23* *And the city had no need of the sun, neither of the moon, to shine in it: for the glory of God did lighten it, and the Lamb is the light thereof. And the nations of them which are saved shall walk in the light of it: and the kings of the earth do bring their glory and honour into it.*

The glory of God is the power source that provides all of the light we will ever need.

## 7. No Night There!

*Revelation 21:25* *And the gates of it shall not be shut at all by day: for there shall be no night there.*

*Revelation 22:5* *And there shall be no night there; and they need no candle, neither light of the sun; for the Lord God giveth them light: and they shall reign for ever and ever.*

Sin and Satan brought darkness. Both are gone, and the Light of the World is now the Light of Heaven!

## 8. No Sin!

*Revelation 21:27* *And there shall in no wise enter into it any thing that defileth, neither whatsoever worketh abomination, or maketh a lie: but they which are written in the Lamb's book of life.*

*Revelation 22:12-15* *And, behold, I come quickly; and my reward is with me, to give every man according as his work shall be. I am Alpha and Omega, the beginning and the end, the first and the last. Blessed are they that do his commandments, that they may have right to the tree of life, and may enter in through the gates into the city. For without are dogs, and sorcerers,* and whoremongers, and murderers, and idolaters, and whosoever loveth and maketh a lie.

Imagine, if you will, a sin-free environment! Once and for all, sin will be eradicated.

Pick up your local paper tomorrow. Go through it page by page and read the stories. As you do, you can say to yourself of every crime, every catastrophe, every sin, every heartache, every obituary — there won't be any of that in Heaven!!!

## 9. No More Curse!

*Revelation 22:1-3 And he showed me a pure river of water of life, clear as crystal, proceeding out of the throne of God and of the Lamb. In the midst of the street of it, and on either side of the river, was there the tree of life, which bare twelve manner of fruits, and yielded her fruit every month: and the leaves of the tree were for the healing of the nations. And there shall be no more curse: but the throne of God and of the Lamb shall be in it; and his servants shall serve him:*

The curse of sin is forever lifted! The new heaven and the new earth will never be touched by the blight of sin. We will be free from the curse of sin in our mortal bodies, and be given a new nature and a glorified body forever absent of sin.

## 10. No More Time!!!

*1 Thessalonians 4:16-18 For the Lord himself shall descend from heaven with a shout, with the voice of the archangel, and with the trump of God: and the dead in Christ shall rise first: Then we which are alive and remain shall be caught up together with them in the clouds, to meet the Lord in the air: and so shall we ever be with the Lord. Wherefore comfort one another with these words.*

*John 3:14-16 And as Moses lifted up the serpent*

*in the wilderness, even so must the Son of man be lifted up: That whosoever believeth in him should not perish, but have eternal life. For God so loved the world, that he gave his only begotten Son, that whosoever believeth in him should not perish, but have everlasting life.*
Let ETERNITY begin!!!

## Points to Ponder and Discuss

1. Of all the things NOT in Heaven, what makes you most glad?

2. Can you think of anything not covered in the lesson that will not be in Heaven?

3. Again, do you know for sure that you are going to Heaven?

# -18-
# Hell & the Lake of Fire (Part 1)

*I cannot preach on Hell unless I preach with tears.*
— D. L. Moody

## Lesson Goals
1. To have our questions answered about Hell and the Lake of Fire
2. To learn the location of Hell
3. To allow God to work in our hearts about the importance of sharing the Gospel with the lost

There are many people alive today who do not believe in the existence of Hell.  However, everyone who is dead does believe in Hell.  Others mock the idea by using hell as a curse word.  Some are so wicked as to boast they would rather go to Hell than Heaven so they can spend eternity partying with their buddies.

It matters little the opinion of men.  What does the Bible say about Hell?

## The Six Most Asked Questions about Hell

### 1.  Is there really a Hell?

*Luke 16:19-31    There was a certain rich man, which was clothed in purple and fine linen, and fared sumptuously every day:  And there was a certain beggar named Lazarus, which was laid at his gate, full of sores, And desiring to be fed with the crumbs which fell from the rich man's table: moreover the dogs came and licked his sores.  And it came to pass, that the beggar died, and was carried by the angels into Abraham's bosom: the rich man also died, and was buried; And in hell he lift up his eyes, being in torments, and seeth Abraham afar off, and Lazarus in his bosom. And he cried and said, Father Abraham, have mercy on me, and send Lazarus, that he may dip the tip of his finger in water, and cool my tongue; for I am tormented in this flame. But Abraham said, Son, remember that thou in thy lifetime receivedst thy good things, and likewise Lazarus evil things: but now he is comforted, and thou art tormented. And beside all this, between us and you there is a great gulf fixed: so that they which would pass from hence to you cannot; neither can they pass to us, that would come from thence. Then he said, I pray thee therefore, father, that thou wouldest send him to my father's house: For I have five brethren; that he may testify unto them, lest they also come into this place of torment. Abraham saith unto him, They have Moses and the prophets; let them hear them. And he said, Nay, father Abraham: but if one went unto them from the dead, they will repent. And he said unto him, If they hear not Moses and the prophets, neither will they be persuaded, though one rose from the dead.*

There is an old adage that says, "If you ask a Bible question, be sure you are given a Bible answer." The Bible answer about Hell is, YES, there is a real, literal place called Hell. Over 50 times, the Bible specifically refers to a real and literal place of eternal torment called Hell.

God Almighty, through His Word, declares 50 times over that there is a real place called Hell, yet the world still scoffs. God paints many pictures of Hell in the Bible – none more graphic than the one found in Luke 16. Some say a picture is worth a thousand words, but I will tell you this – the 299 words found in Luke 16:19-31 paint a thousand pictures of Hell in the mind.

Is there a Hell ? Is it real? Ask the atheist and he

will say "No." Ask the skeptic and he will say, "I doubt it." Take a poll and you will get a statistic. Ask a liberal preacher and he will skirt the issue. Ask the crowd of reprobates in bars and nightclubs on a Saturday night and you will get jokes, clever one-liners and profanity. Ask Almighty God, the Creator of all things, the Author of His sacred book and He will say emphatically, over 50 times – Yes, Yes, YES!!!! There is a real, literal, burning Hell!

## 2. Why would God create a place like Hell?

The Bible Answer: God created Hell for the Devil and his angels.

*Matthew 25:41 Then shall he say also unto them on the left hand, Depart from me, ye cursed, into everlasting fire, prepared for the devil and his angels:*

*Isaiah 14:12-15 How art thou fallen from heaven, O Lucifer, son of the morning! how art thou cut down to the ground, which didst weaken the nations! For thou hast said in thine heart, I will ascend into heaven, I will exalt my throne above the stars of God: I will sit also upon the mount of the congregation, in the sides of the north: I will ascend above the heights of the clouds; I will be like the most High. Yet thou shalt be brought down to hell, to the sides of the pit.*

*2 Peter 2:4 For if God spared not the angels that sinned, but cast them down to hell, and delivered them into chains of darkness, to be reserved unto judgment;*

God originally created Hell for an eventual place of punishment for the Devil and his angels. This supernatural, eternal torture chamber was not intended for men. Lucifer rose up in rebellion against the Lord, and deceived a third of the angels into following him. In response, God created Hell. When mankind sinned, we earned and deserved the same punishment as the devil.

If a man ends up in Hell, he will spend eternity locked up in a place of great evil. He will be out of place in this place! He will be trapped and tortured alongside Satan and devils.

## 3. Where is Hell located?

The Bible Answer: The center of the earth.

*Deuteronomy 32:21-22* *They have moved me to jealousy with that which is not God; they have provoked me to anger with their vanities: and I will move them to jealousy with those which are not a people; I will provoke them to anger with a foolish nation. For a fire is kindled in mine anger,* **and shall burn unto the lowest hell, and shall consume the earth with her increase, and set on fire the foundations of the mountains.**

*Isaiah 5:14* *....hell hath enlarged herself, and opened her mouth without measure: and their glory, and their multitude, and their pomp, and he that rejoiceth,* **shall descend into it.**

*Isaiah 14:9* **Hell from beneath** *is moved for thee to meet thee at thy coming: it stirreth up the dead for thee,*

In Deuteronomy, we see the phrase *"lowest hell,"* and are told that Hell will *"consume the earth with her increase and set on fire the foundations of the mountains."* Isaiah tells us that those going to Hell will "descend into it" and also describes Hell as *"from beneath."*

The story that nails down Hell's location is found in Numbers. A man named Korah decided to challenge the authority of Moses. Notice what the Bible says concerning Korah and his death.

*Numbers 16:29-33* *If these men die the common death of all men, or if they be visited after the visitation of all men; then the LORD hath not sent me. But if the LORD make a new thing,* **and the earth open her** *mouth, and swallow them up, with all that appertain unto them, and they go down quick into the pit;* then ye shall understand that these men have provoked the LORD. And it came to pass, as he had made an end of speaking all these words, *that the ground clave asunder that was under them And the earth opened her mouth, and swallowed them up,* and their houses, and all the men that appertained unto Korah, and all their goods. *They, and all that appertained to them, went down alive into the pit,* and the earth closed upon them: and they perished from among the congregation.

Hell is in the center of the earth. 3,916 miles below our feet are the horrors of Hell. Daily, we walk across the crust of the earth, sadly with little thought of the millions of souls crying out for a drop of water 3,916 miles beneath us. If you are unsaved, you can kneel in repentance and faith and ask for the free gift of eternal life and be saved. But if you die in your sins, you can pray for mercy a million times from the center of the earth and that prayer will never be honored or answered.

3,916 miles might seem like a long way away, but it is not. It is about the distance from Seattle, Washington to Miami, Florida. Yes, Hell is that close.

3,916 miles below your feet, there is a supernatural torture chamber. Everyone you meet today who is not saved is heading there. Keep that in mind this week as you go about your life.

## Points to Ponder and Discuss

1. Why did God create Hell?

2. How close are we to Hell?

3. Whom did God lay on your heart to witness to this week?

# -19-
# Hell & the Lake of Fire (Part 2)

*If sinners be damned, at least let them leap to Hell over our bodies. If they will perish, let them perish with our arms about their knees. Let no one go there unwarned and unprayed for.* — Charles Spurgeon

## Lesson Goals
1. To review what we learned in the previous lesson
2. To understand what is happening in Hell
2. To burden our hearts to reach the lost

## The Six Most Asked Questions about Hell (continued)

### 4. What is Hell Really Like?

In Luke 16:19-31, we read where God gave us an eyewitness account of two men; one who was saved, and one who was lost. The saved man was a beggar by the name of Lazarus. The lost man's name is not given, but because of his great wealth and plush lifestyle, the Bible refers to him as *"a certain rich man."* Both died. Lazarus, upon his death, was greeted and attended to by angels. They escorted him to paradise where the Old Testament saints awaited the resurrection of the Lord. This was a safe place, a blessed place, a place of tender care and divine protection, so much so that it refers to Lazarus' destination as *"Abraham's bosom."*

The rich man also died. No pure angels, no divine servants of God awaited his soul. Instead, that eternal part of him was snatched downward. It happened quickly, with all finality. In one frightening, terror-filled

111

moment, he became aware of his terrible destination as he *"lifted up his eyes in hell."*

Some of what he felt and saw in those first few minutes are recorded as a warning to anyone who would care to read his or her Bible, or who is fortunate enough to find a preacher who still preaches out of Luke 16.

### 1. The rich man instantly becomes aware of the torments.

*Luke 16:23   And in hell he lift up his eyes, being in torments...*

Notice, the word torments is in the plural. Some of these torments are physical, some emotional, some mental. He is tormented by hopelessness. He is tormented as he remembers the chances he had to choose Christ. He is tormented by those he will spend forever with. He is tormented by his own foolish stupidity.

### 2. The rich man notices there is a better place.

*Luke 16:23   And in hell he lift up his eyes, being in torments, and seeth Abraham afar off, and Lazarus in his bosom.*

People who wake up in Hell will come to a quick conclusion:   if there is a Hell, then there must have been a Heaven also!   Not only will they be tormented because of where they are, but also because of what they must be missing.

### 3. The rich man cries out for mercy.

*Luke 16:24   And he cried and said, Father Abraham, have mercy on me...*

The first thing he does is pray. But no prayers will be answered in Hell. The sad thing is, if he would have prayed to God for mercy before he died, then he wouldn't have been here. Now it is too late.

### 4.  The rich man begs for a drop of water.

*Luke 16:24  And he cried and said, Father Abraham, have mercy on me, and send Lazarus, that he may dip the tip of his finger in water, and cool my tongue...*

Another prayer that goes unanswered.  Those in Hell will forever beg for a drop of water, but will never receive it.

### 5.  The rich man is tormented by flames.

*Luke 16:24  ...for I am tormented in this flame.*

Yes, there is hellfire. Hell is a place of real flames and those who go there are tormented by those flames.

*Mark 9:43-44 And if thy hand offend thee, cut it off: it is better for thee to enter into life maimed, than having two hands to go into hell, into the fire that never shall be quenched: Where their worm dieth not, and the fire is not quenched.*

### 6.  The rich man begs for someone to go back and warn his brothers.

*Luke 16:27-31  Then he said, I pray thee therefore, father, that thou wouldest send him to my father's house:  For I have five brethren; that he may testify unto them, lest they also come into this place of torment. Abraham saith unto him, They have Moses and the prophets; let them hear them.  And he said, Nay, father Abraham: but if one went unto them from the dead, they will repent.  And he said unto him, If they hear not Moses and the prophets, neither will they be persuaded, though one rose from the dead.*

No one in Hell wants any of their loved ones to come there.  If we could hear our loved ones who are in Hell, they would beg us to be saved.  They pray someone will share the Gospel with their loved ones who are still alive.  These are the Bible facts.  This is what Hell is really like.

## 5.  Are Hell and the Lake of Fire the Same Place?

*Revelation 20:13-15   And the sea gave up the dead which were in it; and death and hell delivered up the dead which were in them: and they were judged every man according to their works.  And death and hell were cast into the lake of fire. This is the second death. And whosoever was not found written in the book of life was cast into the lake of fire.*

No, Hell and the Lake of Fire are two different places.  Hell, located in the center of the earth, is the temporary holding chamber for the lost until the Great White Throne Judgment.  At that time, Hell will deliver its occupants to stand before God.  All will be judged and all condemned to the Lake of Fire.  Death also, and Hell will be cast into the Lake of Fire at this time.

## 6.  Would a Loving God Really Send Someone to Hell?

Before we look at what a loving God would or would not do, let's look at what a loving God has already done!

1.  A loving God created mankind and gave us a perfect world to live in.

2.  A loving God watched mankind disobey the only rule that God had given him in Eden.

3.  A loving God watched mankind choose sin over paradise.

4.  A loving God could have given up on mankind.

5.  A loving God devised a plan to pay for mankind's sins, so we would not have to go to Hell.

6.  A loving God sent His only begotten Son into the world, knowing His Son would be murdered.

7.  A loving God allowed His Son to be falsely accused, physically abused, spit upon, beaten, whipped, crowned with thorns, mocked, rejected, and nailed to a

cross.

8. A loving God chose not to send legions of angels to stop this treatment of His Son.

9. A loving God then placed the sins of all mankind who had ever lived, was living, or ever would live upon His Son. A loving God allowed His Son – His perfect, holy Son – to become sin for us.

10. A loving God then poured out upon His Son the punishment for the sins of all mankind.

11. A loving God had to hear His precious Son cry out to Him, "My God, my God, why hast thou forsaken me?"

12. A loving God then watched His Son die for you and me.

13. A loving God watched as they put His Son's lifeless body into a borrowed tomb.

14. A loving God sent an angel to that tomb three days later to roll the stone away.

15. A loving God then received His victorious and risen Son into Heaven and welcomed Him to sit at His right hand as the Lamb slain for man's sin.

16. A loving God has provided salvation for all men, a "whosoever" invitation to the human race, and gladly receives and saves all who turn to Him in repentance and faith.

### That is what a loving God did!

Would a loving God send someone to Hell who despises to accept His Son's sacrifice for sin? Would a loving God send someone to Hell who rejects the shed blood of His Son? Would a loving God send to Hell someone who is too proud to admit that he is a sinner in need of what His Son sacrificed? Would a loving God send someone to Hell who, through unbelief, tramples underfoot the precious blood of the Lamb of God?
*YES!*

A loving God would, because He would not be a JUST GOD if He didn't.  And God's justice is never sacrificed on the altar of His love.

In the end, God does not choose to send a lost man to Hell.  The lost man chooses to go to Hell because  he is too proud to humble himself, admit his sinfulness, and call upon Jesus to save him.

## Points to Ponder and Discuss

1.  If we really believed all that the Bible teaches about Hell, would it really seem unreasonable to give our lives to warn people about it?

2.  Whom do you need to witness to?

3.  Are you saved?  Are you sure?

# Summary

I hope, after reading this book, you are never the same. All around you, beneath you, above you — just beyond the limitations of our human sight — exists God's invisible creation.

May we wake each day with a supernatural awareness! With all of our hearts, may we fear our Invisible God, love our Invisible Savior and lean heavily upon our Invisible Companion, the sweet Holy Spirit.

May we be thankful for our invisible helpers, the faithful angels of God, and always sober and alert for the wiles of our invisible enemy. Never underestimate him or his army of devils, but steadfastly resist them by the name of Christ and through the power of His blood.

Every day, let's think upon that heavenly cloud of witnesses cheering us on, and long for the place they now call home. Thank God for Heaven!

At the same time, we must be ever mindful of Hell and the Lake of Fire. Every day, we should speak up for Jesus and try to point men, women and children to the salvation He has made possible for us all.

Ask God to help you see the invisible, so that you can live a life that makes a difference for all eternity.

### 2 Corinthians 4:18
*While we look not at the things which are seen,*
*but at the things which are not seen:*
*for the things which are seen are temporal;*
*but the things which are not seen are eternal.*

# About the Author

Jerry Ross is the pastor of the Blessed Hope Baptist Church in Jasonville, Indiana. He and his wife, Sheryl, have served together in the gospel ministry for over 30 years. In addition to pastoring, Pastor Ross is a popular teen speaker, conference preacher and author.

# A Teenager's Guide Series

*Now available...*

A Teenager's Guide to Character, Success & Happiness

A Teenager's Guide to the Invisible Creation

*Coming soon...*

A Teenager's Guide to Healthy Relationships

A Teenager's Guide to the Local New Testament Church

A Teenager's Guide to Self-Discipline and Organization

A Teenager's Guide to End-Time Prophecy

A Teenager's Guide to Victorious Christian Thinking

A Teenager's Guide to Silent Killers and Besetting Sins

A Teenager's Guide to the Bible and Prayer

A Teenager's Guide to Vibrant Spirituality

*Order by phone: (812) 665-4375*
*Order on the web: www.stayinthecastle.com*